NATIVE AMERICAN AMERICA

North America Before 1492

NATIVE AMERICAN AMERICA

North America Before 1492

ROSEN
PUBLISHING

Tim McNeese, PhD

Published in 2021 by The Rosen Publishing Group, Inc.
29 East 21st Street, New York, NY 10010

Library of Congress Cataloging-in-Publication Data

Names: McNeese, Tim.
Title: Native American America: North America before 1492 / Tim McNeese, PhD.
Description: New York : Rosen Publishing, 2021. | Series: Movements and moments that changed America | Includes glossary and index.
Identifiers: ISBN 9781725342057 (pbk.) | ISBN 9781725342064 (library bound)
Subjects: LCSH: Indians of North America--History--Juvenile literature. | Indians of North America--Social life and customs--Juvenile literature. | America--Civilization--Juvenile literature.
Classification: LCC E77.4 M39 2021 | DDC 970.004'97--dc23

Printed in China

Portions of this book appeared in *The Fascinating History of American Indians: The Age Before Columbus.*

Photo Credits: Cover, p. 3 John Elk III/Lonely Planet Images/Getty Images; p. 7 Alex Erofeenkov/Shutterstock.com.; p. 8 DEA Picture Library/De Agostini Picture Library/Getty Images; p. 9 Culture Club/Hulton Archive/Getty Images; pp. 13, 35 Enslow Publishing; p. 14 Bettmann/Getty Images; p. 15 Warpaint/Shutterstock.com.; pp. 18–19 Private Collection/Wood Ronsaville Harlin, Inc. USA/Bridgeman Images; pp. 22–23 Universal Images Group/Getty Images; p. 27 Billwhittaker at English Wikipedia/Wikimedia Commons/File:Clovis Rummells Maske.jpg/CC BY-SA 3.0; p. 28 Heritage Images/Hulton Fine Art Collection/Getty Images; pp. 30–31 Biblioteca Nacional de Antropologia e Historia, Mexico City, Mexico/De Agostini Picture Library/A. Dagli Orti/Bridgeman Images; p. 33 David Q. Cavagnaro/Photolibrary/Getty Images; pp. 41, 57, 84 Werner Forman/Universal Images Group/Getty Images; pp. 44–45 VW Pics/Universal Images Group/Getty Images; pp. 50–51 DEA/G. Cappelli/De Agostini/Getty Images; p. 53 Transcendental Graphics/Archive Photos/Getty Images; pp. 60–61, 92 Library of Congress Rare Book and Special Collections Division ; pp. 64–65 Stock Montage/Archive Photos/Getty Images; p. 70 Print Collector/Hulton Archive/Getty Images; pp. 76–77, 108 Apic/Hulton Archive/Getty Images; p. 80 Interim Archives/Archive Photos/Getty Images; p. 88 Buyenlarge/Archive Photos/Getty Images; p. 94 Guaxinim/stockish/Shutterstock.com; p. 99 Douglas Peebles/Corbis Historical/Getty Images; p. 105 Universal History Archive/Universal Images Group/Getty Images; p. 109 Joe Sohm/Visions of America/Universal Images Group/Getty Images; pp. 112–113 Three Lions/Hulton Archive/Getty Images; cover and interior pages banner graphic stockish/Shutterstock.com.

CPSIA Compliance Information: Batch #BSR20. For further information contact Rosen Publishing, New York, New York at 1-800-237-9932.

Find us on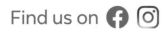

CONTENTS

INTRODUCTION

The fifteenth century was an exciting time in European history. It was the time of the Renaissance, a new social, educational, philosophical, and artistic movement that originated in the Italian city-states, such as Venice, Rome, and Florence. This great wave of change was brought about, in part, by a new level of wealth that was spreading across Europe. Merchants, especially the Italians, were expanding into foreign markets. Europeans were expanding their horizons to greater and greater distances. Traders and merchants competed for the great profits that lay in trade with the Orient. They were trying to gain access to exotic trade goods, such as silks and spices.

Spices were highly valued. All over Europe, people ate food that was less than appealing. There was no means of refrigeration, so food readily spoiled. Meat had to be eaten within a few days of an animal being killed, or it would rot. Europeans had few ways to keep it fresh or to make it taste good. Things were so bad in Europe that many people had become accustomed to having food reach their tables in a semi-rancid state, often just on the edge of spoiling. Taking advantage of overland trade routes, European traders sought eastern markets such as Persia, China, India, and the Spice

A modern spice market in India shows the variety of colorful, fragrant spices available for sale. Centuries ago, Europeans sailed far from home to get their hands on such goods.

Islands in the South Pacific, where they could find every spice from pepper to nutmeg; cloves to spikenard.

All this international trade created new levels of wealth across Europe. Many of the newly made rich merchant class not only put their profits back into additional business efforts, they also sponsored a new emphasis in learning. New schools and educational centers were established. Scholars went in search of knowledge that had been collected in the past, some of which had been lost over time. This led to a newly educated class in Europe, who began looking at the world differently than their contemporaries. Ancient Greek texts suggested that the world was round, not flat. By 1492, a German geographer and mapmaker, Martin Behaim

Fifteenth-century cartographer Martin Behaim created this globe in 1492, before Christopher Columbus sailed west from Spain and discovered the Western Hemisphere. Columbus's discovery made Behaim's globe obsolete.

(1459–1507), built one of the first true round globes. It was a start of a new way of looking at the world.

Behaim's globe had its problems. He created it based on his knowledge of world geography. But what he could not have known was that far to the west, across the Atlantic Ocean, lay an entirely unknown hemisphere—and in it, the Americas. That same year, an important discovery was made. In 1492, an Italian sea captain and mapmaker, Christopher Columbus (1451–1506), attempted to sail to the west to reach Asia and its abundance of spices. What

Based on an engraving by Dutch artist Theodore De Bry (1528–1598), this fanciful print shows Columbus's first meeting with Indigenous Natives on the island of San Salvador, as his men raise a cross in the background.

Columbus would soon learn would change the world and its history forever. Not only did he discover the lands Behaim knew nothing about, he discovered people. They are known today as Native Americans.

1

CROSSING CONTINENTS

Just more than five centuries ago, no one in Europe, Africa, or Asia knew anything about the place known today as the Americas, not even its very existence. They knew nothing about the vastness of its landscapes or of the millions of people who made these lands their home. Thousands of years earlier, groups of ancient peoples had migrated into the Western Hemisphere, the lands that presently make up North, Central, and South America. Over the millennia, the connections between these New World arrivals and the lands they left behind had been lost.

What must it have been like for the first people who found their way to North America? What amazing sights did they see? How did the land they walked on appear? What animals roamed nearby? Were these first people chasing those animals? Or were the animals chasing them? One can never know for certain.

Arrival Theories

There are many theories concerning the earliest arrivals to North America. Sometimes these theories agree with one another; sometimes they do not. While different scientists, anthropologists, and even historians may disagree on which theory is the most likely, they do agree in general on some of the details. However else others might have found their way to the Americas over thousands of years, many arrived by walking from Siberia, the frozen reaches of modern-day Russia, to the New World by a land bridge. During prehistoric times, the landscape of the Americas, especially North America, was different than it is today.[1]

Most scientists, including anthropologists and archaeologists, believe the first humans may have migrated to America during one or both of the two most recent ice ages. During these periods, with more land exposed by low sea levels, the landmass that normally separated North America from the farthest, eastern reaches of Asia was exposed above water. Anthropologists refer to the most recent ice era as the Pleistocene age. This era took place from around seventy-five thousand to approximately ten thousand years ago.[2]

During the Pleistocene era, massive glaciers stood thousands of feet above the landscape as giant ice mountains. These huge glaciers held so much water that sea levels may have dropped as much as 300 feet (91 meters) lower than they are today. The land normally submerged under water between Asia and North America, a waterway known as the Bering Strait, would have been above sea level. Because of this, a large piece of open land extending many miles north and south was opened. The name given to this temporary stretch of exposed land is Beringia. The land was ice-free and thick with lush grasses. These formed a large pasture for animals that migrated into the region. Unlike the modern climate in that part of the world, it would have been somewhat warmer in summer and dry and cold in winter.[3]

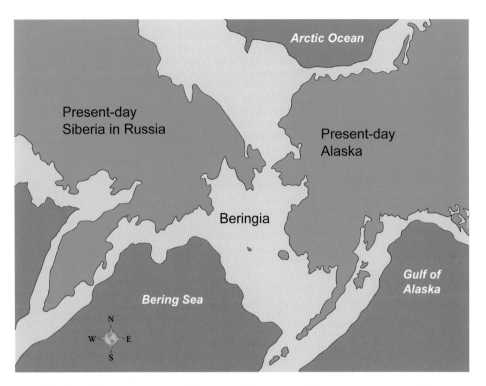

During the most recent ice age, the waters between present-day Siberia and Alaska were lower, exposing a land bridge scientists call Beringia, which allowed ancient people from Asia to migrate into the Western Hemisphere.

It was here that Ice Age mammals migrated, fed, and roamed about. These included Pleistocene horses, camels, reindeer, and bison. The horses were much smaller than modern horses and the bison were massive compared with today's shaggy beasts. These early camels would serve as the ancestors of modern-day llamas found in South America. These animals shared company with others, including musk oxen, saber-toothed tigers, and beavers as large as bears. But above all these Pleistocene era beasts stood creatures of enormous size: mastodons and woolly mammoths.

Mammoths vs. Mastodons

As the name implies, mammoths were immense. They were actually larger than today's elephants! They lived until the end of the Pleistocene era, around ten thousand years ago. Mammoths towered over every other land animal at 10 feet (3 m) in height, and sometimes they were even taller. Mastodons were nearly as large, and, like mammoths, covered in a thick, shaggy coat of hair. Unlike the mammoths, mastodons had oversized, curved tusks. Mammoths had longer tusks, though, measuring as long as 12 feet (4 m)! Just as the mammoths did before them, the mastodons went extinct in North America.[4]

(*Above*) Amid a swirl of Ice Age snow, a pair of Pleistocene mammoths lumber through the rocky landscape. Such great beasts shared the land with other Ice Age animals, such as saber-toothed tigers. Mammoths stood above all other animals at 10 feet (3.05 meters) in height.

(*Left*) Against a great forest backdrop, a lone mastodon readies to take a drink from an Ice Age lake. Mastodons survived frigid temperatures with the help of their thick, shaggy coats of hair.

As the lush grasses of Beringia lured all these animals, large and small alike, out of the continent of modern-day Asia, they continued to migrate, some to the Western Hemisphere and others out of America to the Eastern Hemisphere. They would have done so, of course, without knowing they had left one continent and moved onto another. Paralleling the movement east were ancient humans who followed them, hunting them for food. When the last Ice Age ended, about ten thousand years ago, the sea levels rose once more, leaving Beringia as it had been before—covered with water. This left the animals and the people who had "accidentally" reached the Western Hemisphere as permanent residents of this New World. They continued to hunt and spread out across the landscape of their new continent. In time, the large Pleistocene animals went extinct. No longer did great mammoths tower above the land. The giant beaver, the tiny horses—they all passed out of existence, leaving only their bones to be found by modern archaeologists, anthropologists, and paleontologists. As for the people— perhaps the first to reach the Americas—they settled in to meet the challenges of living in their new environment as the continent's first "Americans."[5]

Early Americans

Today, scientists still know little about the origins of the first humans in the Western Hemisphere. That they came to these unknown lands as migratory hunters seems indisputable. They certainly would have been here as early as twelve thousand to fifteen thousand years ago. But some anthropologists and paleontologists believe the first humans in the Americas reached the continent much earlier than that. True, the most recent Ice Age ended about ten thousand years ago, but another Ice Age occurred before that era. That earlier Ice Age lasted several thousand years.[6]

But just because an earlier Ice Age took place, it does not guarantee that people arrived in the Western Hemisphere during that time. Evidence is necessary to make such a claim. A few anthropologic sites have been excavated, which may point to human life in the Americas prior to ten thousand years ago. Discoveries made in two locations, Daisy Cave in California and Monte Verde in Chile, indicate that groups of people, Asians probably, moved down the Pacific coast of North and South America during a much earlier period of human occupation. Some archaeologists place those coastal migrations as early as 30,000 BCE.[7] The Monte Verde site in Chile may be older than 30,000 years BCE. Tests have been made using radiocarbons to date the site. The earliest such date of human occupation is some twelve thousand five hundred years ago.[8]

But controversy continues to dog these sites. The problem lies in the evidence itself. Although anthropologists have worked diligently at these locations and unearthed such evidence as bones and stones, questions remain. Determining whether a stone or bone artifact was actually worked by a human being at some time in the distant past is sometimes difficult to establish. Therefore, these sites in Western Canada's Yukon, California, Brazil, and elsewhere remain under scrutiny. It may be said, then, that the safest dating of humans in America takes scientists back fifteen thousand years ago.

A Lithic Legacy

Early groups of hunter-gatherers were constantly on the move, following the animals as they migrated from place to place. The primary reason why these peoples were not farmers was that they had lower populations and were expanding into uninhabited country. They had not had a need to develop farming yet. Planting crops in the ground demands that one remain in the same place to bring in a harvest. These ancient peoples were nomadic, meaning they did not settle in a single place for long. As the animal herds moved in search of richer grasslands, small game, fresh water, or to escape harsh weather, so did the clans and families of these early peoples in the Americas. This would be the pattern for prehistoric peoples around the world, from the Americas to Africa to Asia. These Stone Age eras  were, then, universal experiences. Anthropologists identify two significant Stone Ages: the Paleolithic age and the Neolithic period.

Members of a group of Clovis Paleo-Indians follow herds of animals across Beringia eastward over a vast steppe as part of the earliest migration of humans into the Americas.

The first of the two eras, the Paleolithic age, lasted much longer than the Neolithic. It stretched back in time to span, not just thousands of years, but hundreds of thousands. The term "Paleolithic" is used by anthropologists. It comes from two Greek words: *paleo*, meaning "old," and *lithic* meaning "stone." In other words, Paleolithic means "Old Stone Age." In time, the Paleolithic era gave way to the Neolithic age, or "New Stone Age," beginning around 10,000 BCE.[9]

Finding Their Place

While the date for the earliest human inhabitants of the Americas remains a mystery, it is clear that people were in America by the end of the most recent Ice Age, about twelve thousand or thirteen thousand years ago. By that date, the fossil record of early humans becomes clearer. Archaeologists have found evidence of humans living at that time in eastern Siberia and in places scattered across western Alaska. It is assumed that humans also lived in Beringia, but with the end of the Ice Age, Beringia sank beneath the ocean waters as the northern glaciers shrank. Documenting human occupation of Beringia is nearly impossible, since that land has been under water for the past ten thousand years. (Anthropologists have discovered mammoth fossils on the seabed where Beringia was once exposed.)

Once the first humans arrived in America, they began to scatter about, filling in the landscape. The process of migrating to the four corners of the Western Hemisphere did not take place overnight. Scientists estimate that several thousand years passed before humans reached the farthest southern point in South America, Tierra del Fuego.

Working with Stone

Since the lure of the early migrants to the Americas had likely been the animals they were hunting, anthropologists are interested in the weapons they used and how they fashioned them from stone.

While the methods they used to reshape stones into tools differed from one group to another, Paleolithic peoples in the Americas used two general methods. The earliest of the two involved chipping stones called flints to make primitive tools. Using various tools, including stone hammers, antler batons, and smaller antler tips, early toolmakers chiseled away. By working tirelessly, they could reduce a flint core to flakes, then methodically work the flakes into a useful form. Such flakes of flint were chipped, or knapped, into projectile points, hide scrapers, knives, and other tools.

The second method of reworking stone into tools involved pecking and grinding stones. Hard rock types, such as granite or basalt, were reworked into tools by using other stones. Then the ancient toolmaker ground the would-be items against still other stones to produce smooth, even sharp edges. Using this technique, Paleolithic peoples in the Western Hemisphere were able to produce such items as axes, mauls, and metates, or grinding slabs.

Manos (smaller stones) rest beside their accompanying metates (stone slabs). Manos and metates were used by early Native Americans to grind seeds and early crops for easier consumption and cooking.

Evidence exists that humans arrived there and settled around 7000 BCE.[10] People arrived in other parts of the Americas even earlier. By 12,000 BCE, humans had arrived in the eastern portion of the United States.[11] At the Meadowcroft site in Pennsylvania, archaeologists have uncovered human artifacts dating to 15,000 BCE.[12] To the south, the Thunderbird site, located in the Shenandoah Valley in modern-day Virginia, human relics dating to 10,000 BCE have been unearthed.[13]

THE SEARCH FOR NEW WORLD FOOD

Who were these early immigrants to the Americas? What kinds of people were they? Were their lives in the Western Hemisphere different than what they had been prior to reaching the New World? The problem with knowing and understanding the nature of the first people in the Americas is the same as what makes it difficult to identify, and especially pinpoint, a time or date by which they arrived—a simple lack of evidence. Experts can know with relative confidence that those first people who wandered across the Bering Strait land bridge thousands of years ago were an adventurous people. Their very lifestyles demanded it. But they probably did not think of themselves as daring individuals. They were only following the migratory animals of the Pleistocene era. They did not pursue them because they were searching for something exciting in their lives. They had a more primitive and basic reason—survival.

The Door Closes

Regardless of when the earliest humans arrived in the Western Hemisphere, the door of opportunity did not remain open forever. A warming trend brought about a receding of the polar ice cap and a gradual altering of the North American climate. Over the next several thousand years, until approximately 8000 BCE, the Pleistocene era wound down to an end. Most of the animals that disappeared during this period were large ones, ranging from approximately 100 pounds (45 kilograms) in weight to the 4-ton (3.6 metric ton) woolly mammoths. These included the ancient horse and camel, and the saber-toothed tiger.[1]

As the glaciers retreated, North America was transformed. Each part of the continent witnessed new patterns of temperature, seasons, rainfall, and wind. But through all this great change in animal and plant life, one ancient animal did not die out. The Pleistocene era left behind the bison. These shaggy beasts were relatively quick, thus able to outrun humans. With other previously-hunted animals no longer available, early American Indians began to prey heavily on bison and learned to adapt their hunting methods and tools to this fast-moving target. Living in a continuing age of stone, the peoples of North America made changes in how they shaped their tools and weapons.

Clovis Technology

For thousands of years, ancient hunters in the Americas primarily used spears and javelins in stalking their animal prey. A spear is a simple weapon consisting of a long wooden shaft with a stone tip at one end, which anthropologists and archaeologists call a projectile point. (Most nonexperts simply refer to such points as spear points.) These points were fashioned out of stone and used for a variety of tools and weapons. Such points serve as one of the earliest examples of a hand-fashioned tool.

Stone was always serviceable as a durable material to use in making tools and weapons. Not all kinds of rock can be reshaped in something easily by early peoples, so they relied on certain types of stone. They realized early the value of a rock with a sharpened edge. Over long spans of time, they refined their skills in making stone tools, producing such useful items as drills, awls, choppers, and blades of volcanic glass chipped to a razor's edge.

Much of this early stone working was haphazard, with the stone carver never completely certain how each would-be tool would come out in shape or size. However, early craftsmen achieved a breakthrough in stone technology around 10,000 BCE. This new style of working stone produced a highly stylized, extremely functional weapon. It was unique in shape, having both balance and grace. It was a projectile form called the Clovis point. This special point type was found in 1932 in the ribs of a woolly mammoth near the town of Clovis, New Mexico. It would not be until the 1950s that this point was dated using radiocarbon testing. The point proved to date to eleven thousand five hundred years ago.[2]

Ranging in size from 1 to 6 inches (2.54 to 15.24 centimeters) in length, the Clovis point was a bifacial point. This meant it was chipped the same on both faces of the stone so that both sides would be identical. It was also fluted, meaning the base of the Clovis point was flaked to produce a concave trough running about one-third the length of the point, which would accommodate the end of a spear shaft. The shaft end was split into two equal halves, and the Clovis point fit snugly into the split. Ancient hunters then used animal sinew to bind the point to the shaft, producing

These Clovis points represent an important ancient Native American hunting technology. Discovered in present-day Iowa, these points served as deadly weapons for hunting Pleistocene animals such as mammoths.

the most effective weapon thus far for hunting animals of all kinds, including mammoths, mastodons, and ancient camels.

While not a highly technical piece of hunting equipment, the Clovis point nonetheless represents an advance in Stone Age technology. The point was reproduced all across North America. Archaeologists have unearthed examples of Clovis points from New Mexico to Nova Scotia, Manitoba to Montana. Used for approximately two thousand years, its longevity as a tool suggests its power and enduring effectiveness. Its ubiquity and proliferation are markers for archaeologists and anthropologists indicating the population spread across ancient America and the wide dispersal of these early peoples across the American continent by 10,000 BCE.

Early Immigrant Arrivals

Different groups of Asians migrated to the Americas. Anthropologists believe that those who migrated to the Western Hemisphere from Asia and Siberia came in a series of migrations. Those who arrived during the first migration

The Folsom Point

While the Clovis point served ancient hunters well as they tracked their Pleistocene prey, hunting bison ultimately required something new. These hunters needed a weapon they could throw quickly, accurately, and at a higher rate of velocity than the Clovis point allowed. The answer was found in two new weapons.

One was a new style of projectile point. Called the Folsom point, it was first unearthed by archaeologists in 1927 in Folsom, New Mexico. This spear point is different from the earlier Clovis model in several ways. The Folsom is a refinement of the Clovis: smaller, lighter, more delicate, yet deadlier. Like the Clovis, the Folsom is fluted, but the Folsom's fluting extended nearly the entire length of the point. The Folsom was also flaked more finely, giving it a sharper edge than the Clovis. Just like the Clovis point, the Folsom point was mounted on a shaft, but these savvy bison hunters developed an apparatus for hurling these new projectiles. It was a spear-throwing device called an atlatl. The atlatl attached to the end of a shaft could deliver the projectile at a greater speed with better accuracy than earlier spears thrown by hand.

Following the Clovis point, the Folsom point shown here represented an improved hunting weapon.

entered the Americas across Beringia prior to 12,000 BCE. The majority of these migrants remained in northern and western Canada. Another movement of immigrants to the Western Hemisphere arrived late—almost too late. They came around 5000 BCE, long after Beringia was already underwater. Until 2000 BCE, these latecomers, known today as the Inuit, settled all across western Alaska, including the Aleutian Island chain. They extended their settlements across the frozen north of Canada, settling on both the east and west shores of Hudson Bay. In time, these people settled as far east as Greenland. In fact, it would be the Inuit who would make contact with the Vikings, around 1000 CE. The Vikings, European Scandinavians, would represent the next significant phase of migration to America.[3]

Seeds of Agriculture

Beyond hunting and gathering, early American Indians tapped other sources for food. They fished the streams, rivers, lakes, and coastal waters, which were abundant with fish, shellfish, and other marine life. These sources—hunting, gathering, fishing—all served ancient peoples in the Americas well, depending on where they lived.

But in time, early Americans developed a completely different method of getting food for themselves. This method proved to be one they could rely on more readily than hunting or fishing. This was the practice of farming, or systematic agriculture. In the Western Hemisphere, this shift from hunting and gathering first occurred in Mexico.[4] It also occurred in three other places around the globe, starting around 7000 BCE. Each of these four farming regions produced a staple crop. There was Indian corn, known as maize, in Mexico and potatoes in South America.

A diorama shows Mesoamerican farmers harvesting a field of maize, an early ancestor of today's corn, in the southern region of modern-day Mexico. Such agriculture became predominant in the Tehuacan Valley thousands of years ago.

Ancient Bioengineering

As ancient peoples began producing maize, or modern corn, the process was more complicated than one might think. Developing corn took perhaps hundreds of years of reworking an earlier form of plant life, the teosinte grass. Until recently, scientists did not even know of the link between teosinte and the development of corn.

Teosinte is a spindly plant, topped by a line of between five and a dozen small pods, measuring about 3 inches (8 cm) in length. Early Mesoamericans, through their own form of genetic bioengineering, adapted this grassy plant into something resembling modern corn, even if the cobs were a bit smaller.

There was another change in the teosinte plant that helped turn it into a more viable food. Teosinte kernels are hard and difficult to chew without risking breaking a tooth. Ancient farmers, as they adapted the plant, also created a variety that featured softer kernels. Today, the only leftover of those hard kernels is the thin, stringy tissue that often gets stuck between one's teeth when enjoying corn-on-the-cob.

Stalks of corn rise toward the sky, representing thousands of years of bioengineering that began in modern-day Mexico, as early farmers bred the spindly teosinte grass into an ancient corn variety.

And, there was wheat in West Asia and rice in Southeast Asia. These earliest examples of cultivation—the practice of growing crops by planting or scattering seeds in or across a potential field—are often referred to as the Agricultural Revolution, a worldwide phenomenon that would forever change how people lived.

In Mesoamerica (modern-day Mexico), Native Americans grew not only maize, but a wide variety of crops. These included beans, squash, gourds, tomatoes, peppers, and avocados. Central America, including Mexico, was also the source for cocoa (which is used to make chocolate) and vanilla beans. Today, crops such as potatoes and corn are staple foods for hundreds of millions of people in the Americas.

Native American Cultural Regions

By the time of the arrival of Europeans to America in the 1500s, the Western Hemisphere was home to millions of people. How many cannot be said with certainty. Scientists estimate that twelve million lived in North and South America. If that number is correct, it means that one out of every seven people living in the world at that time called the Western Hemisphere his or her home. Such a population would have been equal to the population of Europe at that time. Of the twelve million inhabitants, about 15 to 20 percent, about two million people, lived in North America, including present-day United States and Canada.[5]

These first residents of the Americas began to develop their own unique regional cultures about five thousand years before the arrival of Columbus in 1492. Across what is today the United States, extending north into Canada, seven distinct cultural regions can be identified. By the

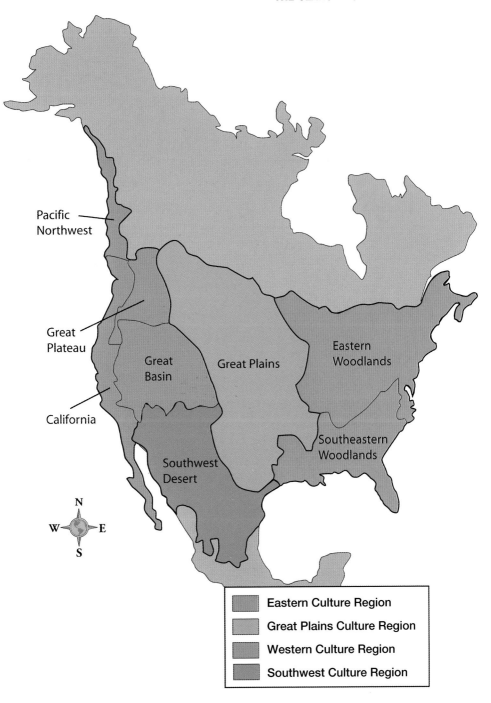

The people of each cultural region in North America developed housing styles, diets, and their general lifestyles as they adapted to their own unique environments.

year 1500, the people of the cultural groups found in each region had developed into distinct nations. The modern first nations, then, were largely in place by the time Europeans begin to arrive. While anthropologists divide the cultural regions slightly differently among themselves, there is a general consensus that at least seven Native American culture regions developed.

The Southwest culture region was centered in present-day Arizona and New Mexico. This region was home to the Navajo, Pueblo, Zuni, and Apache, among others. Some of their homes were permanent sun-dried brick complexes named *pueblos* by the Spanish.

The Eastern culture region extended from the maritime provinces of present-day Canada across the west, including the Great Lakes, and along the Atlantic seaboard from Chesapeake Bay south to Florida, then west to the Mississippi River. Territory stretching from Michigan to Maine was home to the tribes of the region, which included both the Algonquian and Iroquois tribes. Notable tribes of the Southeast included the "Five Civilized Nations": Cherokee, Chickasaw, Choctaw, Seminole, and Creek.

The Great Plains culture region was the largest of the cultural groups. It extended from the Canadian provinces of Manitoba and Alberta to Texas. The region spanned the middle region of the United States from the Mississippi River to the Rocky Mountains. Dozens of tribes were scattered across the region, including the Lakota (the Sioux), Cheyenne, Comanche, and Pawnee.

The Western culture region included two sub-regions, the Plateau and Great Basin. The people there were scattered thinly and included the tribes of the Cayuse, Nez Perce, Bannock, and Shoshone.

The Pacific Northwest culture region was the most uniquely shaped of them all, stretching from Alaska south to British Columbia and Washington State. It hugged the Pacific Coast and rarely extended inland more than 100 miles (161 km) to the east. It was home to dozens of smaller tribes, such as the Clatsop, Haida, and Chinook.

The California culture region also borders the Pacific Ocean, but extends farther east, covering most of the state of California. It was a popular place for Native American tribes to live, possibly one out of seven, although the region only represented 5 percent of the land of North America.

3

PEOPLE OF THE SOUTHWEST

No American region is more mysterious and exotic than that of the Southwest. It is a desert land extending from today's Arizona and New Mexico, and north to include southern Utah, the southwestern corner of Colorado, a sliver of western Texas, southeastern Nevada, and California. The Southwest is a rugged moonscape of painted deserts, snow-covered mountain peaks, and rocky sandstone canyons. Major landforms include the Grand Canyon and the eroded stone monoliths of Arizona's Monument Valley. A dry and arid land, the annual rainfall amounts to less than 5 inches (13 cm).[1]

Early Peoples of the Desert

As the people of the ancient Southwest developed, they produced three types of cultures. They are known today as the Mogollons, the Hohokam, and the Anasazi. Each made a unique contribution to the culture of the Southwest region.

The Mogollon (pronounced muggy-OWN) was located in the southern half of New Mexico and southeastern

Arizona. Mogollon people could also be found in the northern Mexican provinces of Chihuahua and Sonora.

The Mogollons were the first Southwestern people to adopt a culture that included agriculture, the building of permanent housing, and the making of pottery. Their farming included the "three sisters" (corn, beans, and squash) as well as cotton for clothing and tobacco for ceremonial purposes. Like the prehistoric people who settled the Southwest before them, the Mogollon built permanent encampments.[2] By 1100 CE, the Mogollon began constructing adobe structures above ground. Such buildings resembled, to later Spanish explorers, apartment complexes in Spain. Thus, they named the homes of the Mogollon *pueblos*. (The word in Spanish referred to multi-apartment buildings.) Some of these Mogollon villages were home to as many as twenty or thirty such buildings.[3]

At the same time, the Mogollons were flourishing, the Southwest witnessed the rise of another culture group—this one to the west—called the Hohokam. The name comes from the Pima nation of later centuries, who referred to these early people as "hohokam," or "the vanished ones." The Hohokam made their homes in south-central Arizona, in the valleys of the San Pedro, Salt, and Gila Rivers. They practiced a systematic agriculture, built adobe houses, and practiced pottery-making. Their agriculture was so extensive, it provided nearly their entire diet. Their cornfields thrived because the Hohokam were extremely skilled at irrigation. They built water canals and ditches to divert water runoff, and also erected dams on neighboring rivers.[4]

The center of Hohokam culture was located in a community called Snaketown, where the Hohokam lived

Mogollon Pottery

The Mogollon people of the Southwest represented one of the earliest sedentary groups in the region. Since these ancient people grew cotton, they eventually developed into skilled weavers, creating elaborate blankets and clothing complete with feathers and animal furs for adornment. Their pottery was originally a simple style, involving laying coils or ropes of brown clay on top of one another and then smoothing them out and firing them to dry and harden. Then, potters decorated their newly created earthenware. One group of Mogollon people, the Mimbres, developed a highly stylized type of painted pottery which featured black paint on white clay.[5]

A pair of human figures, possibly representing life and death, are used to decorate a Mimbres-style pottery bowl. The Mogollon people punched a "kill hole" in the bottom when the bowls were used as offerings that were buried with the dead.

for fifteen hundred years. The site lies south of modern-day Phoenix, and it featured a hundred underground pit dwellings, larger than those built by the Mogollon.[6]

In the Shelter of the Rock

The third cultural group to develop in the region of the ancient Southwest was the Anasazi. The name means "ancient enemies" in the Navajo language. Anasazi culture began taking shape around 100 BCE and was centered on the "four corners" plateau, where four states—Colorado, Utah, Arizona, and New Mexico—now meet.[7] The Anasazi culture developed through a series of stages. In the earliest stage (100 BCE–400 CE), the Anasazi lived in pit houses. They were hunter-gatherers, yet they also practiced a basic agriculture. They hunted with spears and snares, and used the atlatl to help give their darts and spears greater accuracy and power.[8]

During the second phase of Anasazi culture (c. 400–700 CE), these people lived in pit homes lined with flat stones, covered with wooden timbers and brush. By this era, they had use of the bow and arrow. (Bows were in use among American Indians in modern-day Canada as early as 200 CE. They reached the Great Plains around 550 CE.)[9] They had also domesticated the turkey, and their crops included the three sisters. In the decorative arts, these people produced turquoise bracelets, shell jewelry, and clay effigies, or symbolic figures of humans.[10]

By the third stage of development (c. 700–1100 CE), the Anasazi were building elaborate pueblo systems that were multi-storied, with dozens of rooms connected together, providing small apartments for living space. The upper stories were reached by using wooden-pole ladders.[11]

Eventually, the Anasazi began building new spiritual centers called kivas. These new shelters, or pueblos, were often more elaborate than the underground houses they formerly called home. One of the most elaborate of the pueblos built during this period is found in the desert of northwestern New Mexico, a site called Pueblo Bonito, "the architectural jewel of the canyon."[12]

A City in the Canyon

Centered in Chaco Canyon, Pueblo Bonito was an intricate complex of eight hundred rooms built in the shape of a half-circle. The pueblo rose from the desert floor to a height of five stories. Other structures at Pueblo Bonito include large kivas used for ceremonial purposes. This site may have been home to as many as one thousand people. Chaco Canyon provided these ancient Southwest inhabitants with an ideal setting for desert living. Although the region had little vegetation and few trees, the Anasazi of Chaco created a "center for their civilization—a place where traders exchanged goods and spiritual pilgrimages ended."[13]

Among the most important goods traded at Pueblo Bonito was a single type of stone, which served as the backbone of the desert economy: turquoise. The stone could be mined in New Mexico. To traders from the extensive and advanced civilizations to the south, in Mexico, turquoise was "more valuable . . . than gold or jade."[14] Once the raw mineral was excavated out of regional mines by Anasazi miners and craftsmen, the turquoise was cut into small tiles. Then, through Mesoamerican merchants and traders, the beautiful desert stones were delivered south. There, they would be cut into a variety of shapes and polished for jewelry and other decorative items. For more

Against the stark landscape of the American Southwest, a restored kiva rises out of the ground. This Anasazi kiva, a religious site, is part of the Aztec Ruins National Monument outside Aztec, New Mexico.

than a century, the turquoise trade fueled the economy of Pueblo Bonito. In exchange for goods from California and Mexico, the Anasazi delivered the precious turquoise to those willing to pay premium prices.

One of the hallmarks of Anasazi culture was their engineering abilities. Not only did they construct elaborate, multi-storied apartment complexes and great underground kivas, they also constructed hundreds of miles of desert roads and village streets, which helped connect them to the outside world and to traders. Typically, the Anasazi built their roads in straight lines, opting to cut their paths across almost any natural barrier that stood in their way. With these linear routes fanning out in every direction, the Anasazi built an involved system of signal towers, so that those living in Chaco Canyon would have a means of communicating across wide stretches of desert lands, using signal fires. Since Chaco Canyon did not have all the necessary construction materials the Anasazi needed to build their settlements, these roads were used to deliver such necessities as logs and timber, which had been cut many miles away.

Ultimately, Pueblo Bonito and its outlying communities established a thriving urban complex in the Southwest deserts of today's northern New Mexico. Its one thousand residents utilized eight hundred rooms for their homes, shops, merchant centers, government houses, and social gathering places. A grand plaza sat in the center of the D-shaped village with five story buildings standing above the common meeting grounds. But at the heart of life at Pueblo Bonito was the kiva system. These underground temples can still be found throughout the canyon, but the main complex is located at Pueblo Bonito. Here the

Anasazi delivered many wooden timbers to provide the roof supports for these religious centers. These social and religious centers provided the compass for the settlement, giving them religious direction even as the mysteries of the kiva remained secret from nearly everyone but those who entered into these sunken chambers.

The pueblo building process found at Pueblo Bonito continued into the next Anasazi phase (c. 1100–1300 CE). By this time, the Anasazi had developed into occupation groups that included weavers, farmers, potters, and other craftsmen. Weavers produced cotton fabrics, which were dyed in bright colors and decorated with feathers. During this period, sites such as Pueblo Bonito were abandoned, as their desert culture began to unravel. Several factors caused people in Chaco Canyon to move to other locations. While Chaco Canyon had built up a grand civilization that was both sophisticated and creative, the days of the Anasazi in the canyon were always numbered.[15]

With the collapse of important sites such as Chaco Canyon, the Anasazi did not die out, but simply moved on. Other sites came into use, such as Mesa Verde, located in southwestern Colorado, and Canyon de Chelly in northeastern Arizona. From the Spanish words for "green table," Mesa Verde was built into rock cliffs of the Colorado Plateau. The cliff-side village reached its zenith around 1200 when it was home to approximately five thousand residents.

While the Pueblo Bonito town had been built on an exposed site on the canyon floor of Chaco, the Mesa Verde Native Americans, many of whom probably came from Chaco or were the descendants of those

Causes for Decline

What caused the decline at Pueblo Bonito remains unclear. Archaeologists do know that other groups of people in the Southwest, including those in Arizona and Nevada, began to also trade in turquoise as rivals to Chaco. Perhaps so much turquoise became available that the value of the once-precious stone began to decline. In addition, one of Chaco's most important and longtime markets for turquoise, the Toltec capital in Mexico, Tula, fell into civil conflict, thus cutting off this formerly reliable trade partner. While all these circumstances may have led to the collapse of life at Pueblo Bonito, a natural calamity might have been the greater villain. Beginning about 1130, a fifty-year-long drought cycle set in throughout the region of Chaco Canyon. This drought probably dried up nearly all local water sources. The end result was that by the end of the twelfth century, Chaco Canyon was abandoned, its buildings left to crumble, its turquoise markets having also dried up, as connections with Mesoamerica blew away like a hot desert wind.

who had formerly lived there, built their homes under great rock shelters and overhangs. In its supremacy, Mesa Verde was home to as many as three thousand residents, living in houses sheltered by the rocks, similar to those built at Chaco. Among the largest of these cliff dwellings was one referred to by archaeologists as the Cliff Palace. (Despite its significance today as a major tourist attraction in the southwest corner of Colorado, Mesa Verde was not occupied by nearly the number of Anasazi who lived in nearby Montezuma Valley. Perhaps thirty thousand called that valley their home.) While the canyon overhangs sheltered the villages at Mesa Verde, the lands above the canyon walls were the real centers of economic activity. Here, Anasazi villagers worked the local fields, "reaching their town by climbing the sheer cliff walls with finger- and toe-holds."[16]

By the end of the thirteenth century, the Anasazi of the cliff dwellings began to abandon their homes, the environment proving ultimately too hostile. Examination of tree rings reveals the years from 1276 to 1299 were a part of a drought cycle in the region. The threat of hostile neighboring peoples, such as the Athapascans (the Navajos and the Apache), also drove the Anasazi from their homes. The final era of the Anasazi (1300–1550) was one of transition, as the Anasazi developed into the Native Americans known as the Pueblo. During this period, tens of thousands of Anasazi abandoned their cliff dwellings and established themselves to the east, along the banks of the Rio Grande Valley. Here, they built new towns near water, Alcanfor, Taos, Piro, and others they were still occupying when the Spanish arrived in the region in the 1500s. Still others found new lives to

Passing over an enormous ancient rock shelter, the sun illuminates the ruins of Mesa Verde National Park's Cliff Palace in Colorado. Such complexes were home to hundreds of Native Americans approximately eight hundred years ago.

the west in Hopi and Zuni towns in modern-day Arizona. As the decades passed, the Navajos arrived in the region and took over control of the lands that had formerly been dominated by the ancient ones, the Anasazi.[17]

Modern-Day Pueblo Peoples

When the Spanish explorers arrived in the American Southwest in the 1540s, the written record of the Native Americans living there began. The Spanish named these American Indians the Pueblo, after the Spanish word for village. The name is still used today by the Pueblo people. The term is a general one that refers to the nations known as the Hopi and Zuni of the Colorado Plateau region. Additional Southwestern nations are the Haulapai, Havasupai, and Yavapai groups, desert farmers of central and northern Arizona, as well as the Pimas and Papago, the Navajos, and the Chiracahua, Mimbreno, and Mescalero Apache.

The Spirit of the Village

The Pueblo peoples were not historically led by warrior bands and societies as other regional culture groups were, but instead relied on various religious societies. Each society had a kiva in the village and had responsibility for a specific task, such as hunting, military defense, political leadership, or medicinal cures for diseases. Each society was led by its own priests, who could hand down decisions affecting the entire tribe.

Perhaps the most important religious society of the Pueblos was the Kachina cult. All its members were men and they were split into six divisions, representing north, south, east, west, up, and down. Each division had its own kiva in which to carry out ceremonies and secret rituals.

A 1908 photograph shows a pair of Shooyokos Kachina priests performing in a native Hopi ritual dance in Arizona. Such costumed Kachina represented various Hopi gods or the spirits of the dead.

Kachina priests were responsible for everything related to the tribal masked dances. In most tribes, each Kachina kiva group sponsored three dances annually. These priests were thought to be representations or symbols of either the tribe's gods or the spirits of the dead. They wore masks and elaborate costumes during tribal ceremonies. Each Kachina mask was thought to be so powerful that each one was burned after the death of its wearer.[18]

4

PEOPLE OF THE EAST

One of the important and long-term results of the early Ice Age was how it changed the landscape of much of North America. As glaciers receded, large lakes were formed, including the five Great Lakes. Rivers were carved and the land stretching from the St. Lawrence River in Canada to the Mississippi River and south to the Carolinas attracted many Native Americans. The resulting Eastern culture region created a world centered on water, great forests, and wildlife in abundance.

A Wooded Landscape

The land was originally covered with trees—thick forests of oak, chestnut, maple, and hickory. The early hunter-gatherers used Clovis spear points to hunt the abundant wildlife. About 7000 BCE, the region developed a warmer climate, and a new culture developed: the Archaic. The people of this region became more dependent on deer, nuts, and wild grains for their food. About 3000 BCE, the Native Americans of the Northeast achieved a new level of culture. They planted seeds, growing squash and, out toward the Great Lakes, they farmed sunflowers and marsh elder. Sunflower seeds were ground into flour for bread. The people of this era expanded their fishing and shellfish gathering activities, including catching swordfish off the coast of Maine. In the area of the Great Lakes, these stone-based people began to work with metals, especially copper, which was abundant. They fashioned it into tools, blades, spearheads, and ornaments.[1]

During this Early Woodland Stage, which lasted from 1000 to 100 BCE, the Indigenous people of the Northeast were noted for the building of earthen mounds. The most important mound-building culture was the Adena culture, which eventually developed a highly structured social order. The Adena culture was named for an archaeological site located on the Ohio River in Ohio. They built permanent villages and burial mounds.[2]

A new culture developed called the Middle Woodland. Beginning about 100 BCE and lasting until about 500 CE, the period witnessed another phase of mound building, called the Hopewellian era. During this era, the peoples of the Northeast began planting and harvesting new crops, including tobacco and some maize. They were busy making stone, wood, and metal tools and weapons and constructed large burial sites, burying their dead with their belongings. One Hopewellian grave mound was uncovered by archaeologists and contained sixty thousand pearls.[3]

The people of this era lived in wigwams, oval structures with curved, dome-like roofs. These homes were covered with bark or animal skins. Inside such houses, these Native Americans kept a variety of household items. Hopewellian women fashioned elaborately decorated clay pots to use for cooking and food storage. The men carved stone tobacco pipes in the shapes of animals and human heads, and musical instruments including reed pipes and flutes, drums, and animal rattles.[4]

In the Northeast, from 1000 to the 1400s, just prior to the arrival of Europeans, the people of the region began to develop into the modern nations. These nations include the Delaware, Micmac, Illinois, Shawnee, Narragansett, and the Haudenosaunee, otherwise known by their enemies as the Iroquois.[5]

A Hopewellian pipe is adorned with the effigy of a toad. Such clay pipes were used in ceremonial rituals among the Mound Builders of the Mississippian Culture between 300 BCE and 500 CE.

Building Mounds

The Southeastern culture region of the United States extends west from the Atlantic Ocean to the Mississippi River, and from the Gulf of Mexico north to the Ohio River. These lands provided a home to dozens of Native American groups for thousands of years.

While little is known about the origins of the people of the Southeast, archaeologists do know they were producing pottery in the region as early as 2000 BCE. About 700 CE, a dominant culture rose in the region, which modern archaeologists refer to as the Mississippian culture or the Middle Mississippian. This culture was centered along several key southeastern river systems, including the Illinois, Tennessee, the lower Ohio, and the middle Mississippi. It is thought to be the third in a series of mound-building peoples of the ancient world, preceded by the Adena, Poverty Point, and the Hopewell cultures.[6]

This era of mound builders lasted from 700 CE until the time of the arrival of Europeans along the Mississippi River in the 1500s. When compared to the Adena and Hopewell cultures, the striking difference about the mounds built in the Mississippian period is that these Native Americans built mounds of earthen pyramids. While earlier mounds were apparently constructed as burial sites, the Mississippian pyramids served as temple bases and, occasionally, as the base for a powerful ruler's house.[7]

During the Mississippian phase, a new variety of corn was introduced to the region from Mexico. The Indigenous people of the Southeast continued to practice systematic agriculture. The Mississippians developed major towns and a true city. It was the great Southeastern city of Cahokia (kah-HO-kee-ah), located in the region where the

Mississippi and Missouri Rivers join one another. Cahokia was situated on the eastern bank of the Mississippi River opposite modern-day St. Louis, Missouri. Cahokia was home to approximately twenty-five thousand to thirty thousand people, while an additional twenty-five thousand lived in villages, which surrounded the ancient city.[8]

Archaeologists have unearthed at least eighty-five mounds at Cahokia. Some were as high as a ten-story building. The mounds were built by slave labor, workers who carried basket loads of earth to these sites to build up the ancient mounds. The largest—today known as Monk's Mound—was erected in fourteen stages, from 900 to 1150. The mound covers 16 acres (64,748 square meters) and stands 100 feet (30 m) high. Missisippian culture reached its height of significance somewhere between the eleventh and twelfth centuries CE. By the early 1600s, the ancient Mississippian centers had been abandoned, the population perhaps killed off by starvation, drought, or destruction by an enemy.[9]

The Last of the Builders: The Natchez

Although Cahokia had been abandoned by the arrival of the Europeans in the 1500s, later Mississippian cultures did survive until then, including the Natchez. When the Spanish explorer Hernando DeSoto arrived on the banks of the Mississippi River in 1540, the Natchez numbered about four thousand people living in at least nine town settlements scattered along the great American river.

The last of these mound-building cultures remained relatively intact well into the 1600s. The Natchez were ruled by a powerful king called the Great Sun, who lived in the largest of the Natchez settlements, the Great

Village, located near modern-day Natchez, Mississippi. The belief within the nation was that the Great Sun had descended from the sun, which was considered all-powerful. As a result, the people worshiped the Great Sun, just as groups in Mexico (Aztec) and South America (Inca) honored their exalted rulers.[10]

Daily Life Among the Mound Builders

Daily life among the Natchez centered around agriculture. They produced crops, and the most important among them was maize. In addition, they harvested edible seeds and plants. When the Natchez made first contact with Europeans, they were introduced to a variety of new foods, which became important enough to them that they named their lunar months after them. The thirteen lunar months of the Natchez were Deer, Strawberries, Little Corn, Watermelons, Peaches, Mulberries, Great Corn, Turkeys, Bison, Bears, Cold Meal, Chestnuts, and Nuts. At least two—watermelons and peaches—were brought to America by Europeans.

Natchez houses were rectangular with bent tree saplings used to provide a curving roof. The roofs were covered with thatch grasses. The sides were covered with adobe mud and whitewashed. They were dark because sunlight came in only through the door.

In 1729, the Natchez people revolted against the French who were preparing to destroy the Great Village to make way for a French governor's plantation. The Natchez

In honor of their leader, the Great Sun, Mississippian peoples, called the Natchez, carry him on a special litter. This sketch was done by Antoine-Simon Le Page du Pratz for his 1758 account of the Natchez peoples.

and the French went to war, leaving many on both sides dead. But the Natchez were ultimately defeated. Surviving Natchez were scattered among neighboring nations. However, the descendants of the Natchez and the cultures associated with the Mound-Builders live on. Among those descendants are the Cherokee, Chickasaw, Choctaw, Seminole, and Creek.

While the Native Americans found in the Southeast speak languages derived from several different linguistic

The Family of the Great Sun

The Great Sun was so divine to his people that when he died, his wives, servants, and lodging guards were killed so they could follow him and serve him in the next life. Natchez society was divided into two classes: the nobility (including the Great Sun) and the commoners (everybody else). This lower class of people were called "stinkards" by French explorers and missionaries of the 1600s. Although the two classes were distinctly drawn, it was possible for people from different castes to marry one another. But their children became either aristocracy or stinkard depending on whom their mother was. A noble woman who married a stinkard man would produce noble children. But if a noble man married a stinkard woman, their children were considered stinkards. The Natchez were a matrilinear society, as were other Native American tribes. This meant the children were identified through the mother.

stocks, the majority speak a Muskogean-based tongue. One of the significant exceptions is the Cherokee, who speak a language of Iroquoian base. As with other Native American regions, archaeologists and anthropologists have gathered limited information about the beginnings of Native life in the Southeast region. They do know that pottery was in production by 1000 BCE.

The People of the Longhouse

Even though the mound-building phase of the Eastern Natives faded away, other culture groups continued on, developing into modern Native nations. The Northeast became home to many different Indigenous groups as the Natives had scattered along the coasts, lake country, and river valleys.

The Haudenosaunee Five Nations, the people also known as the Iroquois, lived in present-day Ontario, Canada, and in upstate New York. This group has lived in this region for more than one thousand years. They were among the first of the Northeastern nations to adopt intensive agriculture, shifting away from a reliance on native plants, fishing, and hunting. The Haudenosaunee raised corn, beans, squash, and sunflowers.

The name "Haudenosaunee" refers to the alliance of five Iroquois groups: the Onondaga, Seneca, Oneida, Mohawk, and Cayuga. "The People of the Long House" constructed wooden, bark-covered homes that were, indeed, quite long. On average, the Haudenosaunee longhouses were 50 to 100 feet (15 to 30 meters) long and about 25 feet (8 m) wide.[11] The roof was barrel-shaped, supported by a line of ridge poles running the length of the house. The peak of the house was about 20 feet (6 m) high. Some longhouses were much larger, measuring even 300 feet (91 m) in length![12] Other Northeastern people lived in different housing. The Algonquians built wigwams, which housed fewer people and thus fewer families together. They were much smaller than the longhouses, and designed as bark-covered domes

Haudenosaunee women work at a variety of domestic tasks as men erect a longhouse. Such elongated houses provided homes and shelter for multiple families and were constructed out of long strips of bark.

with a center rising to a height slightly taller than an adult male standing erect. The wigwam might measure 14 by 20 feet (4 by 6 m). Another difference between the longhouse and the wigwam lay in who built each. Iroquois men built the longhouses, while Algonquian women built their wigwams. Several families usually shared the inside the Iroquois longhouse, with two families occupying opposite sides of the house and sharing a single fire site. This was a sign of the importance of sharing.[13]

The confederacy of the Haudenosaunee was a type of democratic league in which every nation had an equal voice. A sixth nation, the Tuscarora, joined in 1713. The League of the Six Nations would serve as an example of New World cooperation among Native Americans.[14]

Some historians believe the Iroquois Confederacy may have provided an example for the organizers of the American system of government that was established after the Revolutionary War, a union of states based on the United States of America's first constitution, the Articles of Confederation.

The Iroquois Confederacy was sometimes known as the Great League of Peace and Power. Along with the longhouse, the confederacy gave the Haudenosaunee their identity. The longhouse was a symbol of their cooperation. Every nation of the confederacy had its special, symbolic place. The Senecas served as the keepers of the western door, while the Mohawks were the keepers of the east entrance. (Iroquois longhouses were situated east to west.) The Onondagas maintained the symbolic fire in the center of the symbolic longhouse. Inside the house, between the Onondagas and the Senecas to the west were the

The Role of Women

Like the nations found in other culture regions in North America, Haudenosaunee families were based on a matrilinear social structure. Such a system places women at the center of family life, with her children born into their mother's family clan. Haudenosaunee women were also able to hold important positions within their group, including that of clan leaders.

Cayugas. The Oneidas were situated in the east wing of the longhouse, between the Onondagas and the Mohawks.[15]

War Among the Iroquois

The Iroquois fought as great warriors when Europeans, primarily the French and English, began arriving by the 1500s. Combat between the Iroquois and other neighboring tribes was extremely violent and bloody. When taking captives, these peoples treated their prisoners one of two ways. They either tortured and killed them, or they tortured and adopted them. The Haudenosaunee believed they gained the power of all those they killed. Typically, a captured enemy was delivered into an Iroquois village as the villagers screamed and howled loudly. Then, the captive was forced to run a gauntlet, two lines of men who struck and cut at the captive repeatedly. For a day or so, the captured enemy was tortured, which might include being burned with firebrands, his skin ripped and cut, as well as other means. The peoples of the Confederacy were noted for these practices by other tribes.

When a captive was killed, his body would be dismembered by the Iroquois women and then cooked. The tribe would hold a great feast with their enemy as the main course. (The Algonquian word for "Mohawk" was "eater of human flesh.") Modern historians believe the Iroquois practiced this gruesome ritual for hundreds of years before the arrival of Europeans to their lands. When the Iroquois adopted a captive (he usually had to show great bravery while being tortured), the adopting family gained his power. Adoptions sometimes took place among the Haudenosaunee to replace a deceased family member, one killed in battle, or a person who might simply have died of disease. Raids launched to deliver captives as tribal replacements were called "mourning wars."

Foods of the Northeast Nations

All Northeastern tribes had a variety of diets, supplied through farming, gathering, fishing, and hunting. Farming among the Haudenosaunee was considered women's work, while the men hunted, caught fish, and traded to distant nations. Farming was not easy for these people since the growing season of the Northeast is short. Hunting was easy in the Northeast, since game was plentiful. The Algonquians hunted deer, caribou, moose, elk, and bear. They also hunted smaller animals, including raccoons, muskrats, porcupines, woodchucks, and beaver, as well as ducks, geese, and grouse.

The Haudenosaunee raised the three sister crops in great variety. They produced sixty types of beans, eight varieties of squash, and many different kinds of corn, including a popping variety, which they mixed with maple syrup. In time, Northeast Nations raised potatoes, pumpkins, and berries, including cranberries and blackberries.[16]

Eastern Native American Mythology

Both the Iroquois and the Algonquians recognized an all-pervasive deity, a spirit that permeated the entire scope of the natural world around them. Though similar in nature, each greater tribal group gave their all-knowing deity a different name. The Iroquois called their great spirit Orenda; the Algonquians referred to theirs as Manitou. These supernatural beings were actually the embodiment of many spirits that lived and occupied all the objects common to each Native American's existence.

Most eastern nations recognized a special class of religious leaders called shamans, who were thought to have great power, including healing the sick. While shamans wielded great spiritual power as tribal holy men, other men filled additional roles as prophets, magicians, and as great healers known as herbalists. Algonquian magicians or sorcerers claimed power over some aspects of the physical world, including the ability to halt the coming of natural disasters.

Healers could be found among the Iroquois as well. Some of their medicine men formed a special group called the False Face Society, whose purpose was not only to heal the diseased, but to keep them from getting sick in the first place. To do this, they carved wooden masks that bore hideous and contorted facial features designed

Iroquois masks, called false faces, typically featured exaggerated features. The wearer usually carved his face out of white pine adorned with horse hair.

to protect the tribe by scaring off evil spirits that carried disease. While each mask was handmade and no two were ever exactly alike, there were about a dozen basic false face designs. Some featured askew mouth formations, others showed tongues protruding, and still others had thick lips and mocking looks.[17]

5

PEOPLE OF THE GREAT PLAINS

In the twenty-first century, it may be difficult for people to picture the world of Native peoples living in America centuries ago. Many, however, have formed their images from old Western movies and television shows. Their stereotype includes such peoples, faces lined with war paint, riding bareback on a mustang while hunting buffalo, living in conical tepees, puffing on a peace pipe, and wearing a large headdress of eagle feathers. Some Native Americans did live this way during the eighteenth and nineteenth centuries, but the image is a limited picture. While not every Native American fits this singular image, the groups it best describes were those who made the Great Plains their home.

A Vast Grassland

The region of the Great Plains is gigantic. It sweeps across the borders of the United States and Canada. Extending from the area of the Mississippi River to the foothills of the Rocky Mountains, the Great Plains were vast, often empty grasslands, today broken up by thousands of farms and ten thousand cities, towns, and villages. From north to south, the Great Plains include three Canadian provinces—Alberta, Manitoba, and Saskatchewan—as well as all or part of more than a dozen states.[1]

The history of the American Indians, which is another term used for Native Americans, of the Plains predates the arrival of Europeans (who introduced the horse to the hemisphere) by many thousand years, as early as eleven thousand years ago. During later centuries, eastern Plains peoples lived in relatively permanent villages and practiced agriculture. Hunting provided an additional source of food.[2]

Life on the Plains

The earliest residents of the Great Plains region were nomadic hunters who lived on the land between eleven thousand and seven thousand years ago. These Paleoindian peoples hunted the great woolly mammoths and ancient bison. Between 5000 and 2500 BCE, the Plains peoples nearly abandoned the region completely, driven both east and west by a warming trend that rendered the Plains inhospitable. The great animals of the Pleistocene era left the region, some becoming extinct, leaving those humans left on the Plains with only smaller animals to hunt, such as the pronghorn antelope.[3]

Around 2500 BCE, people began to return to the Great Plains in increasing numbers. Many came to the Plains from the lands they occupied in the Eastern Woodlands. A new culture developed, the Plains Woodland period, which was firmly in place between the years 500 BCE and 1000 CE. In the midst of that period, sometime between 200 and 400, the people of the Plains had developed a stable, semi-permanent village life in what is today eastern Kansas, Nebraska, Colorado, northeastern Oklahoma, and along the course of the Missouri River from modern-day Missouri to the Dakotas.

These Indigenous people were planting corn and beans for food, while still depending on hunting and gathering wild plants. The use of pottery was in place during these centuries, and tools and weapons were fashioned from stone and bone. A few artifacts were hammered out of copper.[4]

By 900, a new migration of Native Americans from the Eastern Woodlands found their way out onto the Plains, bringing new settlements and villages to the vast expanses of the Eastern Plains. Just as the old villages had been, these new Native American settlements were built along the major rivers of the region. These new arrivals introduced new crops to the region, such as squash and sunflowers. They constructed square or rectangular earthen lodges which were surrounded by a wooden fence or palisade, as was the custom of many nations of the Eastern Woodlands. These Plains Natives hunted bison, driving them over cliffs. This method of hunting bison required an Indigenous runner to lure the bison into following him until he led them to a precipice where they fell to their deaths, while he might jump a short distance to a narrow shelf for safety. While the men hunted, the women practiced farming, using digging sticks to plant seed and hoeing their fields using hoes fashioned from bison scapula, the animal's shoulder blade.[5]

By 1500, a drought on the Plains caused Native Americans to abandon many of their settlements in the western half of the region. About this same time, Plains cultural groups began to make greater contact with one another, although they were separated by hundreds of miles of treeless prairie. New cultures developed and featured larger villages and a greater reliance on agriculture. Villages also became more permanent. Earthen lodges became larger and were now circular rather than rectangular.[6]

The nations that were established on the Great Plains by the time Europeans began reaching their lands, were varied. They included, situated along the lower Missouri River basin, the Iowa, Kansa, Missouri, Omaha, Osage, Otoe, and Ponca. The middle course of the Missouri River was home to the Arikiara, Hidatsa, and Mandan. To the south, across the modern-day state of Missouri, were the Pawnee and to their south, the Wichita.[7]

Living in the Earth

While most people picture the Plains Natives living in tipis, several nations with historical roots in this region did not. One such nation was the Mandan. These people migrated onto the Great Plains around 1100 from the Mississippi Valley and settled in the territory of what is today North Dakota, along the banks of the Missouri River. When the first whites arrived in the vicinity of the Mandan, the nation was living in the Big Bend region of the river. The American explorers, Lewis and Clark, wintered with the Mandan here in 1804–1805.

The Mandan lived in permanent settlements and practiced an extensive agriculture, which included raising corn, beans, squash, sunflowers, and tobacco for ceremonial purposes. They made pottery for storage and cooking. They built their homes in the form of earthen mounds rather than relying on the tipi design. Building a typical Mandan dwelling involved digging a pit measuring one to 4 feet (0.3 to 1.2 m) in depth. This provided the floor for the lodge. A wooden frame was built up from the pit floor, and poles were lashed together, then covered with several layers of

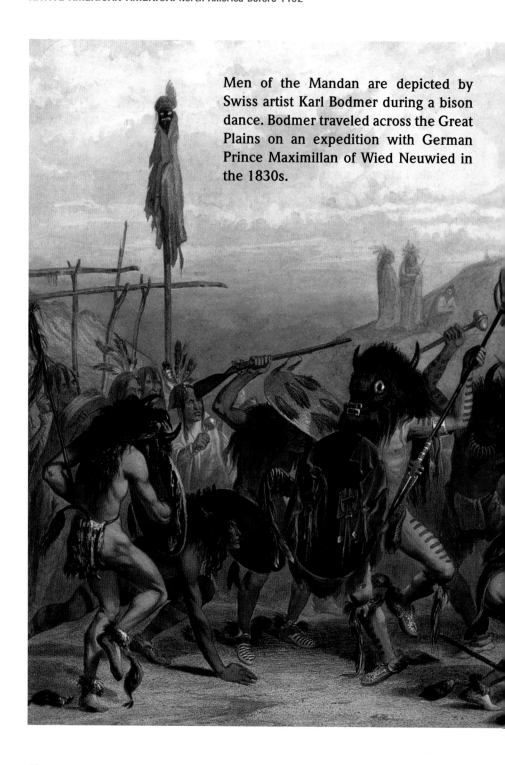

Men of the Mandan are depicted by Swiss artist Karl Bodmer during a bison dance. Bodmer traveled across the Great Plains on an expedition with German Prince Maximillan of Wied Neuwied in the 1830s.

Home for Several Families

Earthen lodges served as home to several families who lived together and often numbered as many as forty or fifty, if not more. Each family provided its own beds, which were placed around the wall of the lodge circle. The lodges also provided shelter for the nation's dogs, and, in cases of severely cold temperatures, even their horses might be housed inside. In the center of the dwelling a fire burned, providing additional warmth for the families living there, as well as heat for cooking. In the center of the roof, the Mandan left a hole for the fire's smoke to escape.[8] In all, eight Great Plains tribal groups lived for at least a majority of the year in such dwellings. In addition to the Mandan, these tribes included the Arikara, the Hidatsa, the Pawnee, the Omaha, the Caddo, the Wichita, and the Osage.

willow branches. On top of this wooden framework, the Mandan placed a layer of prairie grass to provide a roof covering and much needed insulation against the hot summers and frigid winters. Sod was then placed on top of the willow branches and grasses to provide the final roofing layer for the dwelling.[9]

Fighting on the Plains

Warfare on the Great Plains was common between the two dozen nations living across this vast expanse of territory. Plains Natives fighting used a basic organization for warfare: the military society. Males belonged to such groups, typically entering them when they reached their early teen years. These societies imposed a specific code of behavior on their members, requiring them to learn special songs and dances and to wear special insignia, indicating the military society to which they belonged.

While some societies were intertribal, allowing members from different tribes, most were not. Some societies were "closed," allowing only warriors who were invited to join the group. An invitation might be based on a warrior's personal record of exploits and deeds in battle. A nation typically boasted several military societies. The Kiowa had six such societies, including one for young boys, ages ten to twelve, who received early training to become warriors. Originally, the Cheyenne had five societies: the Fox, Elk (or Hoof Rattle), Shield, Bowstring, and the fiercest of all, the Dog Soldiers.[10]

Among the Lakota (Sioux), warriors vied for membership in the elite society known as the Strong Hearts. Within this society, the fighters were called the sash-wearers. Known for their bravery, sash-wearers would advance in the face of an enemy, dismount from their ponies, and stake their sashes to the ground, using a lance. The other end of the sash was tied around their necks. They then fought in this spot, pinned to the ground, refusing to move, until they were either killed or a fellow warrior released them. These warriors were found in other Plains tribes as well, including the Cheyenne.

An 1891 photo captures Kiowa warrior Elk Tongue on horseback wearing an eagle feather war bonnet and carrying a rawhide shield and bow. Tribes on the Great Plains readily adopted the horse during the nineteenth century.

One of the greatest acts of courage a Plains warrior could carry out was the practice of "counting coup." While most cultures that engage in war expect to kill their enemy, the Plains Natives considered it more honorable to humiliate an enemy by merely touching him and perhaps allowing him

The Arrival of the Horse

Once Europeans arrived in the New World during the 1500s, the world of Native Americans soon changed dramatically. One of the best examples is the introduction of the horse.

As the Spanish established their outposts in Mexico and the American Southwest, horses sometimes either escaped or were stolen by American Indians. These powerful animals found their way into their cultures.

The horse changed everything. These animals allowed American Indians to hunt more easily and to even move an entire village from one location to another. With this greater mobility provided by the horse, some Plains nations began to rely less on systematic agriculture as their primary source of food. The result was the development before the end of the 1700s across the Plains of the horse and buffalo culture, something that could never have developed without the arrival of the Europeans in Mexico and the Southwest.

to live. (The word *coup* is French, meaning "blow.") This practice was carried out with a coup stick, which a warrior carried into battle. The stick was not a real weapon but was used to strike or hit an enemy. A warrior could "count coup" on an enemy using a true weapon, such as a bow, a lance, a club, or even just a hand. The purpose of the coup was to show its victim that an enemy was brave enough to come within range of being killed, sometimes armed with nothing but a stick, and that warrior was able to touch his victim without himself being wounded or struck down.[11]

A World of Spirits

To the typical Native American of the Great Plains, the spirit world was a potent place, one which was interconnected with the natural world in which these Native Americans found themselves. Plains Natives religion, as was true of all tribes in the Americas, was by nature animistic. All things—plants, animals, the stars and planets, water, even rocks—had spirits whose qualities could, at least in part, be passed on to warriors who performed certain deeds. For many Great Plains Natives, a practice called the vision quest became an important avenue for making connections between the natural world and the spirit world. Warriors sought visions through an involved series of rituals. Usually, a brave attempted his first vision quest as a teenager. Normally, the process began with the building of a sweat lodge from tree saplings, something similar to a sauna, with the warrior sitting inside. Stones were heated inside the lodge and steam was created by pouring water over the hot rocks. This process purified the brave. He then stripped off his clothing, painting his body with a white clay. Then, he secluded himself outside the camp and fasted for several days.

After days of food and water deprivation, plus continuous exposure to the elements, the warrior hoped to receive a vision, actually an induced hallucination. Such visions were considered a window to the spirit world. If such a vision did not occur, the brave might then cut himself repeatedly, the resulting loss of blood often causing him to become semi-conscious, and thus creating a trancelike state.[12]

Once the vision had taken place, the warrior then often related his dream to a medicine man who served as the vision's interpreter. Whatever was considered to be the vision's most potent symbol—an animal, a tree, a natural element—was then thought to be that warrior's guardian spirit. The brave then began collecting objects to serve as charms, which he recalled from his vision and placed them in a sacred pouch called a medicine bundle.

The Power of the Bundle

These leather pouches were considered powerful medicine to the Plains Natives who carried them. They not only included objects remembered from visions, but other items considered sacred by members of his tribe. Medicine bundles were thought to possess magical powers and brought good fortune to the warrior and his family. While individuals usually carried their own medicine bundles, many Plains Natives bands had medicine bundles of their own. Such bundles were held by tribal chiefs, medicine men, or shamans, and their contents were considered sacred to the entire band or even tribe. Sacred items, such as smoking pipes, often were found among the potent inventory of tribal medicine bundles.[13]

Such medicine pipes were used by the Blackfoot nation and their power was considered important in protecting the tribe. This type of pipe was part of a medicine pipe bundle that was opened and used at the first sound of thunder each spring and again before the onset of winter.

Special Pipes

Pipes were used in many of the ceremonial rituals of the Great Plains tribes. Such pipes were considered holy, sacred, and spiritually powerful. Individuals often made their own pipes, but many nations had pipes that belonged to the entire group. Most pipes were made of wood, sometimes with the stem extending several feet in length. Other pipes were fashioned out of a soft, reddish rock called catlinite. The most important catlinite quarry was located in Minnesota. This quarry was itself considered sacred, and braves from many different nations came to the site. No warfare was to take place on this holy ground and enemies worked within sight of one another, carving out pieces of catlinite to fashion into pipe bowls and stems. While other Plains pipes were fashioned out of steatite or soapstone, these pipes were typically decorated with porcupine quills, feathers, beads and horsehair. Native Americans considered such pipes to be sacred, in part, because the tobacco burned in them was sacred.[14]

6

PEOPLE OF THE WESTERN REGION

The Far Western portion of the continental United States was home to dozens and dozens of Native American nations. But the lands it includes are so different in climate, topography, aridity, and vegetation, the worlds created by those early peoples varied dramatically from one sub-region to the next. From the Rocky Mountains to the Pacific Coast, the American Indians of the West lived in several cultural sub-groups: the Great Basin, the Plateau, Pacific Northwest, and California. West of the Rocky Mountains and east of California's Sierra Nevada lies an American Indian cultural region called the Great Basin. The region is surrounded by vast mountains, including various lower ranges. Since the area is at a lower elevation than its surroundings, it forms a natural "basin" for the region's rainfall. Water has no natural outlet by which to flow out of the Great Basin, so it has historically collected in many lakes within the mountain-locked system. Since rivers and streams drain from the snow-capped mountains into these lakes, the lake water evaporates and then falls as rain once more. This cycle produces lakes of a higher than normal salt content, such as the Great Salt Lake of Utah.

Harsh Life in the Basin

Those American Indians living in the Great Basin have always faced an environment that was hostile and arid. Plant types are few and far between. The region is dominated by juniper trees, sage brush, and pinion trees. Animal life in the region is typically sparse, forcing the occupants of the Great Basin to collect berries, roots, pine nuts, seeds, rodents, snakes, lizards, and grubs. Despite its arid and inhospitable surroundings, archaeologists trace human occupation of the region back to perhaps eleven thousand five hundred years ago.[1]

About nine thousand years ago, the region was home to the desert culture, which relied on hunting. By that time, the large Pleistocene animals had died out. The Indigenous people of this period lived in caves, beneath rock shelters and in wickiups, small huts fashioned from sticks, to protect themselves from the hot climate. Artifacts uncovered from this era include stone and wooden tools, such as digging sticks, wooden clubs, milling stones, and stone scraping tools. Evidence of basket weaving has been unearthed in Danger Cave in western Utah, dating from around 7000 to 5000 BCE. Sometime before a thousand years ago, early Shoshonean-speaking arrivals entered the Great Basin and their descendants have remained there.[2]

Between 2000 BCE and 1 CE, the Basin population had developed into villages, which were typically established near the region's lakes. Adapting further to the surrounding environment, these early villagers engaged in fishing using fishhooks and fishing nets. They also created duck decoys, woven out of local grasses. Hunting was still common, and acorns and pine nuts had become an important part of the local diet.[3] Cactus was harvested for both its fruit

Situated on a barren stretch of desert land, amid outcroppings of cactus, an Apache wickiup provides shelter. Such wickiups were crafted out of native grasses and were meant to be temporary shelters.

and spines. Some cactus fruit was considered sweet and delectable. Cactus needles were roasted.

Among the most important nations of the Great Basin are the Western Shoshone, located in Nevada; the Paiute and Gosiute of Utah; the Washo and Mono of eastern California and western Nevada; and the Northern Shoshone (Wind River) of southwestern Wyoming.

The Abundance of the Plateau

North of the Great Basin lies the region called the Plateau. The Plateau lies between the Rocky Mountains and the

Cascade Mountains of Oregon and Washington states. It extends north into Canada. Other smaller chains give the Plateau an uneven landscape marked by peaks and valleys. The region is also drained by two vast river systems, the Fraser and the Columbia. The great northern bend of the Fraser, located in the Canadian province of British Columbia, forms the northern boundary of the Plateau.[4]

Unlike the Great Basin, the Plateau is a rich region. It comprises portions of eastern Washington and Oregon, as well as the entire state of Idaho, a sliver of northern California, and much of Canadian British Columbia. The Plateau is thick with forests that have, for thousands of years, been home to all kinds of fur-bearing animals such as grizzly bears and beavers, as well as antler-bearing animals,

"Digger Indians"

Agriculture was virtually nonexistent for these American Indians. They remained a gathering people, sending out regular parties of foragers into the greener lower valleys near their villages, collecting seeds, berries, and nuts. They used digging sticks to dig up edible roots. White men who entered the region called the American Indians in the Great Basin "Digger Indians." Just as groups of foragers were formed, the Great Basin tribes practiced regular roundups of rabbits, antelopes, and even grasshoppers for eating. Food remained nearly a constant problem in the arid, bleak environment of the Great Basin.[5]

including deer, elk, antelope, and moose. The rivers, which wind through every corner of the region, teem with fish, including trout and sturgeon. But the prize fish of the American Indians was salmon.

This natural abundance has always been important for these Native Americans, which include approximately two dozen nations. In the southern part of the region are the Klamath, Modoc, Chinook, Salish, Nez Perce, Wishram, Cayuse, and Palouse. To the north, the tribes of the Flathead, Kalispel, Spokane, Coeur d'Alene, Shuswap, and Ntylakyapamuk live beyond the Columbia River. Because of their location in the interior portion of what is today the United States, the Plateau nations did not make contact with Europeans until the 1700s. Even then, the contact was only occasional, consisting of bartering with French and British fur trappers and traders.[6]

The arrivals to this region entered in the southern part of the Plateau, around 4000 BCE. The northern portion of the region saw its earliest inhabitants around 1500 BCE. While the tribal groups of the region find their roots in those two dates, a few peoples arrived earlier than either time frame. Archaeologists have found evidence of Stone Age people dating to the Old Cordilleran culture, who used Cascade points, around 7,500 to 9,500 years ago. By 5000 BCE, a new phase of life developed, the desert culture. With the large Pleistocene animals then extinct, including the mastodons, the Wishram people of the Plateau hunted smaller animals. Basketry came into practice, and milling stones were used to grind food.

About 2000 BCE, the region experienced a shift in temperature patterns, which brought an end to the warm desert culture. Cooler climates brought great snow masses, and greater flow of rivers in the region as well as increased annual rainfall. Now Native Americans began to settle permanently along rivers, and fishing developed as a chief means of sustenance.

The northern forest culture took root by 1000 BCE. This Neolithic culture introduced the region to highly polished, or smoothed, stone tools and weapons as well as copper artifacts. By 1 CE, the Plateau people had developed the Plateau culture, which varied slightly between groups found within the region. During these years, the modern tribal system was developing, and by 500 CE, the tribes of the interior were seriously trading with the nations of the Pacific Coast and with the Great Plains tribes to the east.

Daily Life on the Plateau

Although daily village life varied somewhat from tribe to tribe, the Native Americans of the Plateau shared many common domestic elements. The typical Plateau village might feature a people living together throughout the winter in circular earthen lodges, just as the Mandan and Pawnee did on the Great Plains.

Some tribes built housing that had the appearance of the Haudenosaunee longhouses in the Northeast. These Plateau models were bark-covered and might extend to 100 feet (30.5 m) in length. Such homes were multi-family dwellings and the occupants slept along the outer walls, while a fire burned in the center of the house.

In the summer season, the villagers might live in open-air houses, built of wooden poles and covered with bark, reeds, or rushes. Such homes were usually smaller, single-family structures. Still another summer model of housing used on the Plateau involved a style that used wooden

This 1913 photograph shows men from the Northwest Plateau region in prayer.

planks. These were copied from models found on the Pacific Coast. Such houses were occupied in fishing camps located along rivers and lakes during the summer months. Sometimes such "lake cabins" were built in rows, along the waterfront. At the backs of these Native American houses, the catch of the day, trout and other fish, was hung on racks to dry.

Food was found in abundance, and the Plateau peoples found a bountiful harvest everywhere they turned. They caught fish by spearing and trapping them. Such traps might include a weir, which were placed at the mouth of a narrow river or stream where salmon spawned. The weir featured a barrier built in the stream, much like a fence, which allowed the fish to pass through breaks in the fence, only to find themselves being guided into specially set traps located along a second fence. Fishing was considered a man's job.

Gathering brought an abundant harvest. The Plateau yielded foods that included currants, elderberries, buffalo berries, choke cherries, and serviceberries. The Washo people gathered wild strawberries along the banks of Lake Tahoe and pulverized them into a sweet drink. Bulbs, roots, watercress, clover, even thistle were part of their diet.

California Living

Great numbers of American Indians lived along the Pacific coastal lands as well as further inland in a region known today as the state of California. From the coast to the Sierra Nevadas to the east, this temperate environment was a welcome place for hundreds of thousands of American Indians and scores of independent small nations. But the California culture region is a place of great extremes in topography and, to a lesser extent, climate. It included a

A Special Nut

One of the most important natural products gathered by western range tribes was the pinion nut. The Washoes called the annual harvest Gumbasbai, which meant "big time." The hunt was so important that women first took sacred baths to purify themselves. To gather the crop, women used long poles with hooked tips to shake the tree branches, collecting the nuts in baskets. A group of women and children might gather 1,000 pounds (454 kg) of pinion nuts in just a few days. Pinion nuts were eaten raw, roasted, or ground into flour for baking. In winter, a mixture of water and pinion flour was set outside the lodge and eaten as a Native American version of ice cream.

Pinion nuts were gathered from a variety of pine trees.

northern region with greater rainfall and cooler temperatures year round. But to the south, the California nations lived in a warmer environment, a region consisting of scrubby desert lands, similar to the Great Basin. Yet Native Americans lived there in great numbers. By the time of the arrival of whites to the New World, California peoples may have numbered as high as three hundred fifty thousand.[7] Nearly a hundred nations lived in the expansive region of California. In the north lived the Tolowa, Mattole, Hoopa, Wiyot, and Yurok. These nations sometimes borrowed culturally from the Natives of the Pacific Northwest. In central California lived the Yuki, Karok, Shasta, and Yana. These tribes were similar to those of the Plateau region. Other central Californian tribes included the Patwin, Miwok, Maidus, Yokut, and Wintun. They lived closer to the ocean. To the south, additional nations filled in the landscape, including Cahuilla, Fernandeno, Gabrielino, Juaneno, Luiseno, Nicoleno, Serrano, and Tubatulabal. Many of these nations became known as "Mission Indians" once the Spanish missionaries arrived in the region, bringing with them the Catholic-supported mission system of the late 1700s.[8]

The earliest Indigenous occupants of the California region date as early as twelve thousand years ago. These American Indians were big game hunters who were nomadic. In time, Clovis and Folsom points were used in hunting. By 7000 BCE, one big-game hunting culture, the San Dieguito culture, used chipped-stone tools and weapons and stone-tipped spears. By 5000 BCE, the population of California was already extensive. The dominant culture was the desert culture. With the large animals now extinct, the people gathered seeds and wild plants, and used milling stones to grind food. They also hunted and fished.[9]

Between 2000 BCE and 500 CE, ancient California experienced the Middle Period culture, which featured the use of small canoes and boats to hunt dolphins and other marine animals. These American Indians were more sedentary, building villages while remaining nonagricultural. As with other groups, they harvested acorns as a staple food. During the millennium before the arrival of Europeans (500–1500), the region experienced greater population growth and greater variations of political units. Many nations borrowed culture from the Pacific Northwest, Great Basin, and Plateau tribes. Most of the modern nations were in place by 1300. Throughout centuries of living in close proximity in California, these nations did not go to war over land disputes.[10]

California Lifestyles

The California region is rich in natural resources. The type of foods available varied from tribe to tribe depending on a tribe's location within the region. Tribes in northern California, for example, relied heavily on fish, especially salmon. Just as with other regional Native Americans, such as the Pacific Northwestern tribes, Californians used nets, spears, diverting traps, and fishhooks to catch the fish. Fishermen would build platforms extending out over rivers, spearing the salmon as they leaped out of the water on their way to summer spawning. In addition to salmon, northern California Native Americans caught steelhead, trout, and sturgeon. They also harvested lamprey eels during the spring.

Along the shoreline of the Pacific Ocean, the Native Americans gathered clams, oysters, mussels, and scallops. It was considered women's work to cut open, clean, and dry the fish caught by men, including the salmon, which was typically smoked on large, wooden racks placed over a fire.

The Northwest Culture Group

The Pacific Northwest culture group occupies the smallest region of all the tribes of North America. The region includes an elongated strip of land stretching from the border between modern-day Oregon and California north to the Alaskan coast. This long expanse of land is never wider than 100 miles (45 km) from east to west, hugging the Pacific Coast from beginning to end.

The nations of the Northwest spoke different languages and dialects. Dozens of nations occupied the region since ancient times. Among those American Indian nations recognized were the Haida and Tlingit, who settled in British Columbia; the Clatskanie, Tututni, Chinook, Clatsop, Coos, Kalapuya, Siuslaw, Takelma, and Tsimshian, who lived in coastal Oregon and Washington; and the Cowlitz, Duwamish, Clallam, Skagit, and Lumni, who found their homes farther inland in Washington and British Columbia, settling along various rivers.[11]

Dating the earliest arrivals of Native Americans to the northwest region is difficult. Since the early groups in the region did not use pottery, a traditional means of dating ancient people, archaeologists have relied on various projectile points instead. The earliest occupation in the region, a period called the coastal land hunting period, dates from around 6000 BCE. Hunters used flaked stone-tipped implements of the Clovis variety. It is not until 3000 BCE that anthropologists and archaeologists again pick up the trail. That culture is known as the early maritime, and it was coastal-based, as well as sea-oriented. Inhabitants of the

Northwest used harpoons to hunt sea mammals and slate to make their stone projectile points and tools. These practices were similar to those of the Inuit, who lived further north in modern-day Canada.[12]

Following the early maritime period, anthropologists and archaeologists identify eras of cultural advancement that included new hunting practices both on land and at sea. By 1 CE, the Northwestern cultural practices and values were based on hunting, fishing, and cultivating and gathering wild plants. There was still no systematic agriculture among these peoples. Over the past seven centuries, Northwestern American Indians had developed their intricate social systems and have become extraordinary craftsmen, hewing the various woods of the region into a variety of art forms, tools, and hunting objects, including fancy wooden bowls, gigantic canoes measuring 60 feet (18 m) in length, and totem poles.

The Spirits of the Pole

Totem poles were typically carved from cedar and served several purposes for their owner, depending on the type of pole. The most common totem pole was the memorial pole, which American Indians erected to note the rise in power of a family member to noble status. Another pole variety, the mortuary pole, was often placed near the grave of a deceased leader. At the top of such poles, a container holding the ashes of a cremated chief might be placed. Yet another type of pole was the potlatch pole, carved to further the prestige of a family after they had hosted a special ceremonial gathering and feast called a potlatch. But the most common totem pole was called the house pole. These highly symbolic poles were raised either outside the

This portion of the Kadjuk Bird Totem Pole shows the figure of Raven at the top along with Fog Woman, the wife of Raven, who is holding a pair of salmon, a mainstay of the Native American diet in the Northwest culture region.

front door or inside the home and proclaimed the family's status to all who passed by or entered.[13]

Totem poles featured a variety of animal-spirit creatures, or totems, that were stacked on top of one another. Such poles might depict an eagle, killer whale, wolf, raven, the mythical beast called a thunderbird, or the monstrous bird, Hokhokw, whose long beak was powerful enough to crush a warrior's skull. Including a particular animal in a totem pole was a way for a wealthy person to pay his respects to the spirit of the animal.[14]

Northwestern Abundance

By the time of the arrival of the first Europeans in the Pacific Northwest, the tribes of the region were densely populated and their social orders were highly complex. Due to the abundance of food, trees, animal and sea life, the Natives of the Northwest became some of the wealthiest found in North America. They developed rich economies that caused these Native Americans to become accustomed to having property and the social prestige that wealth brings.

What caused the Native Americans of the Pacific Northwest to become so expectant of wealth? What allowed them to accumulate so many material goods while other Indigenous regional groups lived basic lives of subsistence? The answer lies in their environment.

Nature was abundant in the Pacific Northwest region. The forests were homes to gigantic trees; lakes and rivers were full of fish; and living along the ocean coast gave the people there access to a rich harvest of marine life, including whales. The result was a lifestyle that reflected this abundance. The Northwest tribes hunted, fished, and gathered so much food that it was rarely a problem.

Hunters stalked elk, bear, deer, caribou, and other woodland animals for food, fur, sinew, and bone. There was always plenty, giving the tribes of the Northwest a rich diet and the opportunity for great wealth.

And the chief source of food for the region's Native Americans was salmon. This great fish could be found by the millions in the icy waters of the Northwest. Because it was, and still is, a creature of habit and instinct, the fish was an easy one to catch. Each year, during the summer, salmon made spawning runs up every available water source in the Northwest. When the salmon were "running" upstream, whole tribes would abandon their villages and fish through this annual season.

Another source of bounty for the Northwestern tribes was the immense red cedar trees found in the region. Because of the heavy rainfall, these cedars grew to great heights, providing the raw material for many of the material goods of the Northwest. Native Americans made their homes out of cedar planks. These were some of the most elaborate, roomiest homes built by Native Americans.

Cedar is a finely grained wood, which provided the Native Americans of the region with an easy carving wood. They fashioned elaborate cedar canoes, tools, weapons, baskets, and domestic items such as wooden dishes, bowls, and great cedar chests. These chests held the abundance of blankets accumulated by a wealthy chief.

Spiritual Lives

The religious acts of prayer, experiencing visions, and curing the sick dominated the spiritual lives of many of the American Indians of the Western region. Chief among the religious leaders of many of these tribes were the specially designated spiritualists called shamans. These medicine men bore the responsibility of curing the sick members of the group. Great Basin religion relied heavily on the concept of the spirits, which might influence their lives, as well as a reliance on the powers of shamans and special dances. Not only could shamans heal, but they could also curse. Shaman spirits could be cast on a human being, causing physical and mental illness, even delirium.

The supernatural beings found in Northwestern mythology are a combination of both helping spirits and those who do evil or mischief. Men and women called on the spirits to give them blessings in nearly everything they did, from hunting and going to war, to carving a canoe or making a basket. Those seeking help from the gods approached them in a variety of ways, including prayers, incantations, and charms. They also took pilgrimages to sacred places, such as lakes, rivers, mountains, and valleys. They also approached their shamans who might serve as go-betweens, since they were seen as the nation's members with the most direct connections to the spirit world.[15]

As for California Native Americans, their religion included rituals and denying themselves certain foods or activities. They recognized the power of their gods. California Nations also believed that their daily physical lives could make contact with the spirit world. These American Indians practiced many different ceremonial rituals that helped them mark the passing days of the calendar by recognizing the changing seasons. These nations of Californians believed in a number of gods. Each god had control over a given aspect of a person's life. Californians believed that, through their rituals, they were recognizing the power of their various gods.

7

RIVALS IN THE NEW WORLD

Today, the name Christopher Columbus is one of the most famous in the world. Through his efforts, Europeans were reintroduced—Norsemen had reached North America five centuries earlier—to the Western Hemisphere. While Columbus did not truly "discover" the Americas (after all, when he arrived in 1492, millions of people already called North, Central, and South America their home), he did permanently alter the course of history.

Sighting a New Land

Early on the morning of October 12, 1492, European sailors sighted a land they had never seen before. They were part of a Spanish flotilla of only three small wooden ships. They had sailed across the Atlantic Ocean under the sponsorship of Ferdinand and Isabella, the king and queen of the Spanish Empire. Christopher Columbus was the captain of these ships of discovery. Before the end of the day, Columbus and his men would reach the shores of an island in the Bahamas. With their arrival in the Americas, the New World, the history of the world would never be the same.

Ironically, Columbus had not been searching for the lands he landed on. He had been attempting to sail west to reach the Far East, with its valuable spices, silks, hardwoods, and other treasures. During the months that followed his October landing in the Caribbean, he remained convinced he had arrived in what was then called the "Indies." (Today, they're known as the West Indies.) So certain was the Italian sea captain of his success that he called the people he made contact with "Indians."

A Legacy of Exploitation

Columbus attempted to establish a Spanish colony in the Caribbean during his first voyage across the Atlantic. But those first colonists were killed after treating the local island peoples poorly. When Columbus returned that same year on his second voyage, with more than a thousand eager colonists under his command, the Spanish were not guaranteed their colonizing efforts would succeed.

Violence would break out as the Natives attempted to remove the unwanted Spanish presence. Then, the well-armed Spanish, with their muskets, armor, dogs, ships, and cannons, would put down their attacks and crush all resistance. The Spanish would then control all aspects of Native life, turning the Native Americans into slaves, forcing them to work in their own mines, and making them pay tribute to the new power in the New World: the Spanish conquistadors, soldiers who were well-armed and ready to use their might against a simpler foe. Over and over, Spanish conquerors left a trail of blood and destruction among their American Indian victims.[1]

The numbers tell the harsh story. Throughout the 1500s, for example, the estimated Native population of Mexico, twenty-five million, was reduced to one million. But the destruction of the Native population was not primarily

In the 1500s, Spanish conquistador Hernán Cortés and his soldiers managed to subdue the Aztec due to such advantages as guns, steel swords, and armor, including helmets.

caused by war. Instead, disease was the primary killer. European diseases, introduced through simple contact, laid waste to entire groups of American Indians. Smallpox, measles, diphtheria, typhoid, and a list of plagues and fevers ran unchecked through Native populations. Native Americans did not have natural immunities to such new diseases. Once smallpox arrived in the Caribbean in 1518, one out of every three Indigenous people on the island of Hispaniola died within one year. The following year, measles struck, killing even larger numbers than smallpox. Twenty years later, the island's Native Taino population numbered only a few thousand. The year before Columbus's arrival on the island, the Tainos had numbered approximately one million.[2]

The Columbian Exchange

An additional aspect of exchange between Native Americans and Europeans was food. Colonists discovered and took back to Europe such new foods as the potato, squash, pumpkin, corn, and tomato. American cotton also proved better than Asian types. In return, the New World saw its first lemons, coffee, sugar cane, wheat, oranges, rice, and lettuce.

Animals were also exchanged. The horse was introduced to Native Americans, as well as cows, chickens, sheep, and pigs. These provided new sources of meat, hides, and wool, changing Native cultures forever. New World tobacco became widely used in Europe and other parts of the world. Two great tastes also made their way to Europe through vanilla beans and cacao.

Cultural change became the norm for American Indians between the sixteenth and nineteenth centuries. Sometimes,

Other European Influences

During the centuries that followed the arrival of the first Europeans to the New World, American Indian culture groups continued to struggle. Additional European powers found their way to America—the French, British, Dutch, Portuguese, and Swedes—with each establishing colonies on Native American occupied lands. In some cases, these new European groups found ways to cooperate with American Indians. The French established an extensive empire based on trading furs with the Native nations, resulting in a long period of cooperation and mutual benefit. But in most cases, when Europeans arrived to take their place on American soil, it would mean the uprooting of Native populations. The result was that Native Americans typically lost their land and their security and suffered the destruction of their cultures.

the changes were positive for the Native Americans. Certainly, Native groups benefited by adopting the horse into their cultures. Indigenous people also adopted firearms, as well as metal tools and weapons from the Europeans. While such adoptions might improve Native lifestyles, they also changed Native cultures. By switching to iron cooking kettles, some Native nations stopped making pottery. By adopting the horse, the people of the Great Plains became more mobile. This led some to nearly abandon agriculture and to become more reliant on hunting bison. Change for American Indian populations was constant.

Karl Bodmer's artwork of a Blackfoot warrior on horseback holding a rifle shows how Native Americans adopted aspects of European culture into their own societies.

And with those changes, Indigenous culture moved into a new era. The worlds the Native Americans had created for themselves, after thousands of years of adapting to life in the Western Hemisphere, were altered. And what were the achievements of those Native peoples prior to the arrival of Columbus and all those who would soon follow after him to the New World? American Indians had established clear political and social systems. In some cases, the leaders were the women, rather than the men. In the Northeast, women

Cultural Blending

Many modern-day Native Americans still retain aspects of their ancestors' ways of life. In Central and South America, thousands of twenty-first century Indigenous people still live "in pre-Columbian style dwellings and [favor] the same foods their ancestors ate hundreds of years ago."[3] Across the American Southwest, Pueblo Natives live in adobe and stone houses that their ancestors built centuries ago, even as their windows have glass and the furniture inside their homes had been bought at a store. Outside their ancient adobes, they park their cars and trucks. To the north, in Alaskan waters, modern-day Inuit still fish in

During a ceremonial dance held in Gallup, New Mexico, a Zuni Pueblo woman balances a piece of pottery on her head.

the same waterways their people have fished for more than a thousand years, though their boats ply those waters using outboard motors.

served as the heads of individual family units as well as clans. Women also chose which men would be allowed to sit on tribal councils. All this indicates an open-minded approach to leadership practiced by some American Indians prior to the arrival of the Europeans.

They had established extensive systems of farming, growing large fields of crops ranging from corn to beans to squash. Indigenous people had established extensive trade routes and had worn down long trails that crisscrossed the various regions of modern-day America. Many of those Native American trails and paths would one day become the routes for modern American roads and highways. American Indian religions were well defined by the arrival of the Europeans. They engaged in longstanding rituals, cult practices, and worship practices, including dances, songs, and prayers. The Indigenous world of 1492 was a crazy quilt of different cultures stretching from North to South America. These cultures were, typically, highly complex and well-established. The world of the American Indians was as advanced as any that had ever existed since the arrival of the first human beings in the Western Hemisphere thousands of years earlier.

CONCLUSION

Today, the Western Hemisphere is still home to the millions of descendants of Native Americans similar to those who greeted the new European arrivals. Even across five hundred years of time, modern-day Native Americans continue to feel the impact of having been "discovered" by Europeans. Since October 12, 1492, "Indians [have] been uninterruptedly on the defensive, fighting for their lives, their homes, their means of sustenance, their societies, and their religions."[1] Throughout the past five centuries, millions of Europeans have found their way to the New World. They built homes, purchased or stole lands, and established new societies and nation states. Throughout those centuries, the original inhabitants of the Americas have struggled to survive. Epidemics of diseases carried by Europeans raged through Native towns, killing millions. Constantly, they engaged in battles of war with whites, sometimes winning the battles, but rarely winning the wars. Slowly, but with a die-cast certainty, American Indian cultures were forced to give way to the advance of the non-Natives. Treaties might be agreed upon along the way, but those paper agreements were often broken by the whites.

Puritan missionary John Eliot preaches to a group of Massachusetts Natives, circa 1650. Eliot was instrumental in translating the Bible into their language.

Yet American Indians have managed to survive. For many of today's American Indians, their lives are a combination of the old and the new. Almost from the beginning, Europeans expected the Native Americans to adapt to their presence, to assimilate, or become like the Europeans themselves.

Europeans and their descendants, including the majority of the residents of the United States, believed their cultures were superior to those of the American Indians. After all, they had guns and large ships; they had special skills and their favored crops and livestock. They believed they had a better religion, Christianity. The new arrivals to the New World were determined from the outset to turn the New World into their world. Native Americans were often forced to adapt or perish.[2]

Indeed, America's Indians did learn many of the ways of the Europeans. Indigenous people eventually accepted the concept of private individuals owning parcels of land. They changed their clothing styles, learned to eat new foods, and became skilled in European and American crafts and other trades. Many converted to Christianity. Throughout the centuries, they would become farmers, ranchers, blacksmiths, soldiers, shopkeepers, sailors, ironworkers, factory workers, and office workers.

The lives of many of the American Indians of the twenty-first century continue to straddle two worlds—the modern and the traditional. Although they have changed, having altered many aspects of their daily lives through a thousand changes delivered to them by white men, they continue to keep one foot firmly planted in tradition. Their history, those long-lost eras of time and space, when their earliest ancestors hunted the lands with stone-tipped spears, fished ancient waters, prayed to their eternal gods of sun and moon, planted their maize, and formed whole societies based on blood and family, remain a never changing touchstone for today's American Indians.

CHRONOLOGY

25,000 BCE Humans may have reached the Yukon, indicated by evidence found at the "Old Crow" site.

15,000 BCE Earliest claim of humans at the Meadowcroft rockshelter site in Pennsylvania.

13,000 BCE–10,000 BCE Early humans reach the Americas by crossing Beringia.

12,000 BCE Prior to this date, the first wave of migrants to the Americas, the Amerinds, takes place.

10,000 BCE The Neolithic era begins. Clovis points are used by ancient hunters; the second wave of migrants to the Americas, the "Na-Dene," begin arriving.

9000 BCE Humans arrive in the eastern portion of the modern-day United States; the earliest inhabitants of the Southwest have arrived.

8000 BCE The Pleistocene era ends; it marks the end of the use of Folsom points.

7000 BCE Early humans may have reached the southern tip of South America; Plano points have replaced Folsom points; in modern-day Mexico, Indigenous people are engaging in systematic agriculture.

5000 BCE The Native cultural group known by anthropologists as the "Red Paint People" are established along the northeast coast of North America.

5000 BCE–2000 BCE The third wave of migrants to the Americas, the Inuits, reach the Western Hemisphere.

2500 BCE Natives of the Southwest begin cultivating maize.

1000 BCE Village life is established in modern-day Mexico.

100 BCE Southwestern people are making early forms of pottery; Anasazi culture begins to take shape.

1000 BCE–500 CE The Early Woodland Stage: Indigenous people of the Northeast build earthen mounds.

300–900 The peak period for Mayan culture in Central America.

650 The urban culture group, the Toltecs, is established in central Mexico.

700 Polynesians settle on Easter Island, 200 miles (322 km) from South America.

700–1100 The third phase of Anasazi culture, the Developmental Pueblo period, witnesses the building of elaborate, multi-storied pueblos.

1100–1400 The peak period for the culture of the Mogollons and Hohokams in the Southwest.

1200 The Anasazi culture at Mesa Verde reaches its high point.

1492 Christopher Columbus ushers in the arrival of Europeans into the New World.

1500 The vast majority of Native American tribal groups have been established and continue into modern times.

CHAPTER NOTES

CHAPTER 1

Crossing Continents

1. J. M. Adovasio with Jake Page, *The First Americans: In Pursuit of Archaeology's Greatest Mystery* (New York, NY: Random House, 2002), pp. 45–47.
2. Arrell Morgan Gibson, *The American Indian: Prehistory to the Present.* (Lexington, MA: D.C. Heath and Company, 1980), p. 10.
3. Jake Page, *In the Hands of the Great Spirit: The 20,000 Year History of American Indians* (New York, NY: Free Press, 2003), p. 19.
4. Page, pp. 36–38.
5. Carl Waldman, *Atlas of the North American Indian* (New York, NY: Facts on File Publications, 1985), p. 1.
6. Alvin M. Josephy Jr., *The Indian Heritage of America* (Boston, MA: Houghton Mifflin Company, 1991), p. 37.
7. Michael Lemonick and Andrea Dorfman, "Who Were the First Americans?" *Time*, March 13, 2006, p. 48.
8. Page, p. 25.
9. Hugh Thomas, *A History of the World* (New York, NY: Harper & Row Publishers, 1979), p. 11.
10. Josephy, p. 271
11. Josephy, p. 83.
12. Adovasio, p. 157.
13. Brian M. Fagan, *Ancient North America: The Archaeology of a Continent* (New York, NY: Thames and Hudson, 1995), pp. 114, 117.

CHAPTER 2

The Search for New World Food

1. Jake Page, *In the Hands of the Great Spirit: The 20,000 Year History of American Indians* (New York, NY: Free Press, 2003), p. 37.

2. Charles C. Mann, *1491: New Revelations of the Americas Before Columbus* (New York, NY: Vintage Books, 2006), pp. 167–170; Page, pp. 22–23.

3. Alvin M. Josephy Jr., *The Indian Heritage of America* (Boston, MA: Houghton Mifflin Company, 1991), p. 47.

4. Hugh Thomas, *A History of the World* (New York, NY: Harper & Row Publishers, 1979), pp. 19–22.

5. Peter Charles Hoffer, *The Brave New World: A History of Early America* (Boston, MA: Houghton Mifflin Company, 2000), p. 38.

CHAPTER 3

People of the Southwest

1. Alvin M. Josephy Jr., *The Indian Heritage of America* (Boston, MA: Houghton Mifflin Company, 1991), p. 147.

2. Josephy, p. 152.

3. Josephy, p. 152.

4. Jake Page, *In the Hands of the Great Spirit: The 20,000 Year History of American Indians* (New York, NY: Free Press, 2003), p. 73.

5. Page, p. 80.

6. Page, pp. 73–75.

7. Alvin M. Josephy Jr., *500 Nations: An Illustrated History of North American Indians.* New York, NY: Gramercy Books, 1994, p. 56.

8. Josephy, *Indian Heritage*, p. 156.

9. Brian M. Fagan, *Ancient North America: The Archaeology of a Continent* (New York, NY: Thames and Hudson, 1995), pp. 136, 181.

10. Josephy, *Indian Heritage*, p. 157.

11. Josephy, *Indian Heritage*, pp. 158–159.

12. Josephy, *Indian Heritage*, p. 58.

13. Josephy, *Indian Heritage*, p. 57.

14. Josephy, *Indian Heritage*, p. 58.

15. Josephy, *Indian Heritage*, pp. 158–59.

16. Josephy, *500 Nations*, p. 61.

17. Josephy, *Indian Heritage*, pp. 159–160.

18. Nancy Bonvillain, *Native Nations: Cultures and Histories of Native North America* (Upper Saddle River, NJ: Prentice Hall, 2001), p. 349; Barry M. Pritzker, *A Native American Encyclopedia: History, Culture, and Peoples* (New York, NY: Oxford University Press, 2000), pp. 5, 33.

CHAPTER 4

People of the East

1. Alvin M. Josephy Jr., *The Indian Heritage of America* (Boston, MA: Houghton Mifflin Company, 1991), pp. 83–86.
2. Josephy, pp. 86–87.
3. Josephy, pp. 88–89.
4. Josephy, pp. 89, 92.
5. Nancy Bonvillain, *Native Nations: Cultures and Histories of Native North America* (Upper Saddle River, NJ: Prentice Hall, 2001), p. 37; Barry M. Pritzker, *A Native American Encyclopedia: History, Culture, and Peoples* (New York, NY: Oxford University Press, 2000), p. 399.
6. Josephy, p. 103.
7. Josephy, p. 103.
8. Alice Beck Kehoe, *North American Indians: A Comprehensive Account* (Upper Saddle River, NJ: Pearson, 2006), p. 160; Jake Page, *In the Hands of the Great Spirit: The 20,000 Year History of American Indians* (New York, NY: Free Press, 2003), pp. 70–71.
9. Kehoe, pp. 160–162.
10. Josephy, p. 106.
11. Pritzker, pp. 400, 438.
12. Joy Hakim, *The First Americans* (New York, NY: Oxford University Press, 1993), p. 51.
13. Josephy, p. 92; Page, pp. 166–167.
14. Arrell Morgan Gibson, *The American Indian: Prehistory to the Present.* (Lexington, MA: D.C. Heath and Company, 1980), p. 66.
15. Page, p. 164
16. Josephy, p. 92.
17. Pritzker, pp. 437–438, 449, 467.

CHAPTER 5
People of the Great Plains

1. Alvin M. Josephy Jr., *The Indian Heritage of America* (Boston, MA: Houghton Mifflin Company, 1991), p. 111; Barry M. Pritzker, *A Native American Encyclopedia: History, Culture, and Peoples* (New York, NY: Oxford University Press, 2000), p. 291.
2. Josephy, p. 111.
3. Josephy, pp. 111–112.
4. Josephy, p. 112.
5. Josephy, p. 113.
6. Josephy, p. 113.
7. Josephy, p. 114.
8. Nancy Bonvillain, *Native Nations: Cultures and Histories of Native North America* (Upper Saddle River, NJ: Prentice Hall, 2001), pp. 182–183.
9. Bonvillain, pp. 182–183.
10. Josephy, pp. 119–121.
11. Jake Page, *In the Hands of the Great Spirit: The 20,000 Year History of American Indians* (New York, NY: Free Press, 2003), 210.
12. Pritzker, p. 293.
13. Arrell Morgan Gibson, *The American Indian: Prehistory to the Present.* (Lexington, MA: D.C. Heath and Company, 1980), p. 244; Pritzker, pp. 293, 298.
14. Pritzker, pp. 293, 298.

CHAPTER 6
People of the Western Region

1. Alvin M. Josephy Jr., *The Indian Heritage of America* (Boston, MA: Houghton Mifflin Company, 1991), p. 125.
2. Josephy, pp. 126–27.
3. Josephy, p. 127.
4. Josephy, p. 131.
5. Josephy, p. 128.
6. Josephy, p. 136.

7. Josephy, p. 138.
8. Josephy, pp. 138–139.
9. Josephy, pp. 139–140.
10. Josephy, p. 141.
11. Josephy, pp. 73–74.
12. Josephy, p. 74.
13. Arrell Morgan Gibson, *The American Indian: Prehistory to the Present.* (Lexington, MA: D.C. Heath and Company, 1980), pp. 84–85; Barry M. Pritzker, *A Native American Encyclopedia: History, Culture, and Peoples* (New York, NY: Oxford University Press, 2000), p. 164.
14. Josephy, pp. 77–78.
15. Gibson, p. 85; Pritzker, pp. 163–164.

CHAPTER 7
Rivals in the New World

1. Peter Charles Hoffer, *The Brave New World: A History of Early America* (Boston, MA: Houghton Mifflin Company, 2000), pp. 85–87, 89; David J. Meltzer, *Search for the First Americans* (Washington, D.C.: Smithsonian Books, 1993), pp. 8–9.
2. Hoffer, p. 84.
3. Alvin M. Josephy Jr., *The Indian Heritage of America* (Boston, MA: Houghton Mifflin Company, 1991), p. 346.

Conclusion

1. Alvin M. Josephy Jr., *The Indian Heritage of America* (Boston, MA: Houghton Mifflin Company, 1991), p. 346.
2. Arrell Morgan Gibson, *The American Indian: Prehistory to the Present.* (Lexington, MA: D.C. Heath and Company, 1980), pp. 237, 270; Peter Charles Hoffer, *The Brave New World: A History of Early America* (Boston, MA: Houghton Mifflin Company, 2000), p. 2.

GLOSSARY

anthropologist A scientist who studies the cultures of humans, both contemporary and ancient.

archaeologist A scientist who studies historical remains and sites.

assimilate To adapt or change one's culture by taking on the culture of another group.

atlatl An ancient, hand-held device designed to increase the velocity of a spear, as well as its killing power.

Beringia The temporary land bridge spanning the modern-day Bering Strait. During prehistoric ice ages, Beringia provided land passage for migratory animals and human hunters from Asia into the Western Hemisphere.

Bering Strait The body of water that today separates the easternmost point of Russian Siberia from the western edge of Alaska.

Clovis point A stone projectile point used by primitive hunters about 11,500 to 10,000 BCE. The point is known for its limited fluting, or troughing, to accommodate a spear shaft. Clovis points were used extensively in North America.

Folsom point A stone projectile point used by primitive hunters about 10,000 to 8000 BCE. It is smaller, lighter, more delicate, yet deadlier than the Clovis point. Like the Clovis, the Folsom is fluted, but the Folsom's fluting extended nearly the entire length of the point.

ice age A geological period of time when a large percentage of Earth's water is locked in ice causing a lowering of the oceans and seas worldwide.

kiva A circular chamber built underground by ancient Southwest Nations and used for ceremonial and religious purposes.

mastodon A large, extinct mammal with long, curving tusks that was similar to but genetically distinct from the mammoth.

matrilineal Identifying children's ancestry through the mother, rather than the father.

metate An ancient grinding slab fashioned from stone by Native Americans.

paleontologist A scientist who studies prehistoric plant and animal life.

Renaissance The era of European history from 1300 to 1500, during which Europeans began to explore the oceans, change their art, expand their economies, and establish important monarchies across Western Europe.

rockshelter A natural overhang of rock along a cliff wall that provided shelter for early human beings from the natural elements.

three sisters The three primary crops raised by many early Indigenous agriculturalists: corn, beans, and squash.

Western Hemisphere The lands that include North, Central, and South America, as well as the islands of the Caribbean.

West Indies An early geographic term used by Columbus and other Europeans to identify the lands of the Caribbean.

wickiup A type of Native American shelter in the form of a small hut fashioned from sticks.

zenith The highest point.

FURTHER INFORMATION

BOOKS

Birmingham, Robert A., and Amy Rosebrough. *Indian Mounds of Wisconsin.* Madison, WI: The University of Wisconsin Press, 2017.

Childs, Craig. *Atlas of a Lost World: Travels in Ice Age America.* New York, NY: Pantheon, 2018.

Do All Indians Live in Tipis? Questions and Answers from the National Museum of the American Indian. Washington, DC: Smithsonian Books, 2018.

McNab, Chris. *Warriors of the Plains Tribes.* New York, NY: Cavendish Square, 2018.

McNab, Chris. *Warriors of the Southwestern Tribes.* New York, NY: Cavendish Square, 2018.

McNab, Chris. *Warriors of the West Coast, Plateau, and Basin Tribes.* New York, NY: Cavendish Square, 2018.

Sapp, Rick. *Native Americans State by State.* New York, NY: Chartwell Books, 2018.

WEBSITES

DesertUSA
www.desertusa.com/ind1/du_peo_paleo.html
Dive deeper into the history of the earliest inhabitants of North America.

National Park Service: Mesa Verde
www.nps.gov/meve/
Read more detailed information on the people and places of the Mesa Verde site.

Yukon Beringia Interpretive Center
www.beringia.com/

Learn more about the Beringia land bridge, Ice Age animals, and the first peoples that migrated to the Americas.

FILMS

America Before Columbus (2016), National Geographic.

Ice Age Columbus: Who Were the First Americans? (2005), Discovery Channel.

Native America (2018), PBS.

INDEX